HISTORY OF THE CURTINS

3rd Edition

D.P. Curtin

Dalcassian
Publishing
Company
PHILADELPHIA, PA

Library of Congress Cataloging-in-Publication Data

Copyright © 2021 Dalcassian Publishing Co.
In affiliation in Barnes & Noble Press
All rights reserved.

CHAPTER I

Origins of the
Clan MacArtán

c. 11th century to the 17th century AD

The following volume is an attempt to explore the genealogy of the Curtin family based upon the available genealogical information that has survived the centuries. This is not to say that this is all encompassing, nor does it represent all Curtin families. There appear to be at least three different origins of the Curtin families who hail from County Cork. They are: 1) the Dal gCais who are descendants of the ancient kings of Munster, and who gained renown as ancient Ollams in the court of the Kings of Thomond well into the 18th century, known as "macCruithins". 2) the O'Curtins of Cork, who allegedly hail from Ballymaccurtin and who appear to be heavily dispersed throughout the region as early as the 17th century. 3) the Curtins/MacCurtains who are discussed in this work, who are reluctant transplants from Ulster following the end of the Nine Year War.

The earliest origins of the Curtin line can be found in the O'Hart Pedigree of the Irish nation. However, it is clear from O'Harts work that many generations are missing between the 4th and 10th century, as there are large gaps in the identifiable characters. For that reason, these early and largely pre-historical personalities are omitted from this line, as well as the semi-mythical characters noted in Milesian genealogies. Instead, characters that have both surviving historical characteristics and are distinctively linked the formation of a separate Macartan line, differentiated from the more familiar Maguiness clan.

It is also worth noting that this is not exhaustive. This test is laid out in two separate articles, one for the ancient origins of the clan, and a second article exploring the various primary and famous branches. This author has taken measures to stop genealogical tracts and abridge them at certain point as to make this work more readable for common use. There are large number of Curtin descendants who are not mentioned here for the sake of brevity. The descendants of Curtin Clan abide in both Ireland and on foreign shores, such as France, Australia, Canada, Great Britain, and the United States, as well as mixed into various nations of Latin America. Additionally, this author has discerned not to include any living person into this text to protect too much information being available to the general public.

Moreover, this volume should not be regarded as definitive, as it represents a growing collection of information regarding the origins of the Curtin Clan. It certainly rests on the back on the vast advancement of technology, wherein so many otherwise obscure documents are now available to the public and having informed this text.

It has been my sincerest honor to have composed this volume and be granted the opportunity to cast light on what has been otherwise forgotten by the passing of time. It has been the fate of the Irish nation, and much of Irish America, to have lost of much of its past because of calamities and invasions that have damaged the collective memory of the nation. To be able to restore the memories of this, my native clan, through my research has been the magnum opus of my academic work, which I am more then happy to present to you here.

D.P. Curtin
Glen Mills, PA
January 22, 2021

1)   Artán macCruinneith,
Ancestor of the Macartan Clan

His name can be rendered as 'Arthur' in its English transliteration, a common Celtic name, albeit infrequent in Ireland. For more practical purposes it appears to be a battle moniker, meaning "the bear" in Gaelic. He is the alleged progenitor of the clan Macartan according to the O'Hart national pedigree. O'Hart renders previous generations, but there is a large gap of a few centuries prior, which make all prior generations largely dubious in terms of their historicity. Little is known of his life from surviving chronicles. His birth date and name is unknown, he allegedly received the name 'Artan' after supporting Brian Boruma, 175th High King of Ireland in his attempt to consolidate power in Ulster. He was likely born between 960 and 97 AD. He is mentioned being killed in 1004 AD by Flaighbertach at the battle of Loch Bricran. There he is described as being the heir of Ui Eatach, and therefore the proprietor of large sections of Ulster. His wife's name is not mentioned in any surviving text, although she was likely tied to the Ui Niall dynasty which held political dominance in the region throughout the 10th and 11th century. He had at least two sons:

> i)   **Muíreartach macArtán** (*Murdock Macartan*), he is
>   said to be among the first to assumed MacArtán as a

surname. According to the Annals of the Four Masters he was King presumptive of Iveagh (County Down). He was killed at the Battle of Mullachs in 1011 AD. He has no known issue.

ii) **Cuonincon macArtán**, (*See Generation 2 below*)

i) **Artán macArtán**, who is mentioned as a child in the History of Clanna-Rory. It is possible that no such person existed and that this was simply an ancient scribal error.

Irish Soldiers in Ulster, circa 1100

2) Cuonincon MacArtán,
son of Artán

Chief of the Macartan Clan, King of Cíneal Fógartaígh

He was King of Kinelarty according to O'Hart, although this appears as an anachronism. He may have held the title of Chief of the Cíneal Fógartaígh and certainly held sovereignty over the region that surrounds modern Co. Down. His name is render multiple different ways in the surviving sources: Cuonicon, Onchon, Craobharcan, Onchu, Craolchu, and Conchobhar. Any attempt to decipher its meaning appears fairly fruitless. His wife is unknown, but he was father to at least one son:

    i)   **Crum na-Cruach macCuonincon MacArtán**, (*See generation 3 below*)

3) Crum na-Cruach macCuonincon MacArtán, (*Crum the Bloody*)

son of Cuonincon MacArtán, son of Artán

He is also ancestor of the Crokes, Crookes, and Stacks according to O'Hart's Irish Pedigrees. He also likely held the title of Chief of Cíneal Fógartaígh. The use of his name is curious, as Crum Dubh was the 'black deity' of pre-Christian Ireland. Its use in the 11th century was peculiar. The post-nomen 'na-Cruach' can be translated several ways. It be understood as "of the Hills", or "the Bloody", or "Stalks". He is not noted in ay surviving chronicle, nor are there are later legends regarding his lifetime. Nothing else is noted regarding his life. Father to at least one son:

    i)   **Concruach macCrum MacArtán**, (*See Generation 4 below*)

---

4) Concruach macCrum MacArtán, (*Conn of the Hills*)

son of Crum na-Cruach MacArtán, son of Cuonincon MacArtán, son of Artán

Little is noted of Concruach in any record beyond O'Hart's genealogy. Like his grandfather there appears to be some confusion of how his name is to be transliterated into English. The sources call him: Concruach, Con Cruach, Cuchranach and Cuchruach. From this it might be assumed that the original name was 'Conn Cruach', or 'Conn of the Hills'. His wife is unknown, but he was father to at least two sons:

    i)   **Eochaid macConcruach MacArtán**, (*See Generation 5 below*)

    ii)   **Eocha Oge macConcruach MacArtán**, this name is curious as it implies that there was another Eocha. However, O'Hart provides not genealogy for this. It is possible that Eocha was the birth name of Artan.

5) Eochaidh macConcruach MacArtán,

son of Concruach MacArtán, son of Crum na-Cruach MacArtán, son of Cuonincon MacArtán, son of Artán

Chronologically we can date his lifetime to around 1035-1075 AD. The lifespan of these early generations appears unclear given there are very few earmarks to determine their lifetime. We have little to nothing regarding the events of Eochaid's life itself. If he did hold sovereignty over the rest of the Macartan clan it was unknown, as many of the chieftains recorded are given no proper name. Moreover, his name was extremely common in pre-Norman Ireland, making it impossible to offer any additional information regarding his identity. His wife is not recorded, but he was the father of two sons:

    i)   **Dermot MacArtán**, Chief of the Cíneal Fógartaigh (Kinelarty). In 1152 AD he aided in the founding charter of the monastery of Newry, along with Múirchertach Mac Loughlin, High King of Ireland[1]. According to the Annals of the Four Masters he died in 1165 AD, just

---

[1] O' Laverty Rev James, History of the Diocese of Down and Connor, (James Duffy and sons London 1887) 5 vols vol1, p82 London 1887

before the Norman invasion. He is said to have been a crusader, possibly during the militarily unsuccessful Second Crusade. His return from Jerusalem was unanticipated by the local denizens of Ulster, who thought him lost to the distant campaign in the Levant. His stone grave in Newry stood until the Cromwellian invasion.

ii)   **Searran MacArtán**, (*See Generation 6 below*)

6) Searran macEochaidh Macartán,

Eochaidh son of Concruach MacArtán, son of Crum na-Cruach MacArtán, son of Cuonincon MacArtán, son of Artán

Chief of the Macartan Clan, King of Cíneal Fógartaígh

The Clan Macartan appears to have been interested in repulsing the Anglo-Norman invasion under King Henry II. While Searran is not mentioned by name, the last High King of Ireland, Rúaidrí Ó Connor, attempted to siege the Norman fortification of DeLavy in Co. Meath in 1174 AD. Participating in this venture were the Chiefs of Connaught, but also by Ó Neill of Cínel Eóghain, Múrchadh, Ó Ceargháill, Mac Duínnsléibhe and the McCartans[2]. Their efforts were largely unsuccessful and would go on to set the tone for the Macartan's relations with the Plantagenet administration in Dublin for the next four centuries. However, this appears to have been short lived, as the autonomous of Cineal Fogartaigh developed over the next century. His wife is unknown, but he was father to at least one son:

      i)   **Bugmaille macSearran Macartán**, (*See Generation 7 below*)

---

[2] Orphen, G.H., The Songs of Dermot and the Earl, (Oxford 1892)

Irish Kingship ceremony, 12th century, by Gerald of Wales

7)   Raghnall macSearran Macartán,
(Ronald Curtin)
son of Searran son of Eochaidh son of Concruach MacArtán, son of Crum na-Cruach MacArtán, son of Cuonincon MacArtán, son of Artán

He is called Raghnall in all sources, saving only O'Hart who calls him 'Bugmaille', an otherwise unknown name. 'Ronald' is the English equivalent of this name. He likely lived between 1100 and 1180. Nothing is known regarding his life or his political dealings. Given the limited information granted about him in the annals, he either died young or had no political contemporary involvements. He had at least one son:

      i)   **Ciannait macBugmaille Macartán** *(Kenneth Curtin)*, *(See Generation 8 below)*

8)   Ciannait macBugmaille Macartán

(Kenneth Curtin),
son of Raghnall son of Searran son of Eochaidh son of Concruach MacArtán, son of Crum na-Cruach MacArtán, son of Cuonincon MacArtán, son of Artán

Chief of the Macartan Clan, King of Cíneal Fógartaigh

His name is the old Gaelic variation of 'Kenneth'. He is said to have perished in the military campaign to drive the Norman Lord Sir John DeCourcy from Downpatrick. DeCourcey had engaged in a military campaign to pacify the region for Angevian rule. In early January of 1177, he sent an army of 22 knights and three hundred foot-solders against the coalition forces of the King of Ulster, whom Ciannait was vassal to. Ciannait died in June 1177 AD[3] after being confronted with this army, although the battle where he was killed is unknown. DeCourcey went on to conquer much of the region, dispossessing the Gaelic gentry at well. He did this without the permission of King Henry II. He appears to have had to make some submission under the newly formed Earldom of Ulster. Ciannait also likely held the title of Chief of Cíneal Fógartaigh sometime during his life. He was likely born around the year 1110. He had at least one son:

> i)   **GilColumba macCiannait Macartán**, *(See Generation 9 below)*

---

9)   Giolla Colm macCiannait Macartán

(GilColumba Curtin)
son of Ciannait son of Raghnall son of Searran son of Eochaidh son of Concruach MacArtán, son of Crum na-Cruach MacArtán, son of Cuonincon MacArtán, son of Artán

His Gaelic name "Giolla Colm" translates to 'the servant of Columba'. He is estimated to have been born around 1135 AD. Nothing is known regarding his life. Given the pre-nomen attached to his name, it is unlikely that he held sovereignty over the region at any point. He had at least one son:

> i)   **Domnall macGiolla Colm Macartán** *(Daniel Curtin),* *(See Generation 10 below)*

---

[3] O' Laverty Rev James, History of the Diocese of Down and Connor, Davidson, vol1 p82. Reprint 1987

10) Domnall macGiolla Colm Macartán

(*Daniel Curtin*)

son of Giolla Colm son of Ciannait son of Raghnall son of Searran son of Eochaidh son of Concruach MacArtán, son of Crum na-Cruach MacArtán, son of Cuonincon MacArtán, son of Artán

He also likely held the title of Chief of Cíneal Fógartaígh. He is only mentioned in O'Hart's pedigree. According to the Annals of Loch Ce, he died in 1242 AD[4]. He had at least one son:

    i)   **Eochaid macDomnall**, (*Eochy Curtin*), (*See Generation 11 below*)

---

11) Eochaid macDomnall Macartán

(*Eochy Curtin*),

son of Domnall son of Giolla Colm son of Ciannait son of Raghnall son of Searran son of Eochaidh son of Concruach MacArtán, son of Crum na-Cruach MacArtán, son of Cuonincon MacArtán, son of Artán

He is only mentioned in the History of Clanna-Rory, and in the pedigree of Dubhaltach macFirbisigh. Nothing else is known about his life. He had at least one son:

    i)   **Cinnait macEochaid**, (*Kenneth Curtin*) (*See Generation 12 below*)

---

12) Cinnait macEochaid Macartán

(*Kenneth Curtin*),

son of Eochaid son of Domnall son of Giolla Colm son of Ciannait son of Raghnall son of Searran son of Eochaidh son of Concruach MacArtán, son of Crum na-Cruach MacArtán, son of Cuonincon MacArtán, son of Artán

Cinnait is estimated to have been born in 1185 AD. He is only mentioned in the History of Clanna-Rory, and in the pedigree of Dubhaltach macFirbisigh. Nothing else is known about his life. He had at least one son:

    i)   **Giolla Colm macCinnait**, (*GilColumba Curtin*) (*See Generation 13 below*)

---

[4] Annals of Loch Ce, A Chronicle of Irish Affairs 1014-1599, Ed by W.M. Hennessy (Rolls Ser 1871)

13) Giolla Colm macCinnait Macartán

(GilColumba Curtin),

son of Cinnait son of Eochaid son of Domnall son of Giolla Colm son of Ciannait son of Raghnall son of Searran son of Eochaidh son of Concruach MacArtán, son of Crum na-Cruach MacArtán, son of Cuonincon MacArtán, son of Artán

Cinnait is estimated to have been born in 1210 AD. He is only mentioned in the History of Clanna-Rory, and in the pedigree of Dubhaltach macFirbisigh. Nothing else is known about his life. He had at least one son:

    i)   **Donnchadh macGiolla Colm,** *(Donough Curtin) (See Generation 14 below)*

    ii)   **Fionnach macGiolla Colm**, *(Finock Curtin)* He is mentioned by O'Hart, who appears to be confused to which brother is the father to Sean Macartan.

---

14) Donnchad macDomnall Macartán

(Donough Curtin),

son of Giolla Colm son of Cinnait son of Eochaid son of Domnall son of Giolla Colm son of Ciannait son of Raghnall son of Searran son of Eochaidh son of Concruach MacArtán, son of Crum na-Cruach MacArtán, son of Cuonincon MacArtán, son of Artán

Chief of the Macartan Clan, King of Cíneal Fógartaígh

Donnchad must be the Macartán chief who was summoned by Henry III, Lord of Ireland in his war against Alexander II, King of the Scots in 1244 AD[5]. He is said to have died in Scotland. Little is known about his life beyond the historical references. He had at least one son:

    i)   **Sean macDonnchad Macartán** *(John Curtin),* (See Generation 15 below)

---

[5] Calendar of Documents relating to Ireland 1171-1307, Ed by H.S. Sweetman and G.F. Handcock (Record Pubs) 5 vols 1875 -188

Woodcutting of skirmish between English and Irish forces, 14th century

15) Sean macDonnchad Macartán

(*John Curtin*),
son Donnchad of son of Giolla Colm son of Cinnait son of Eochaid son of Domnall son of Giolla Colm son of Ciannait son of Raghnall son of Searran son of Eochaidh son of Concruach MacArtán, son of Crum na-Cruach MacArtán, son of Cuonincon MacArtán, son of Artán

Chief of the Macartan Clan, King of Cíneal Fógartaígh

He is estimated to have been born around the year 1260. He was likely the same Johannes MacCartan noted as succeeding Echmhildh Magennis as king of the Irish of Uibh Eatach in 1333 AD[6]. He also appears to have played a role in the regional rebellion following the death of William, Earl of Birmingham in 1334 AD[7]. Chronologically he must be one of the chieftains who ambushed Edward Bruce, during the Scottish invasion of Ireland in 1316[8]. The sources describe the chief simply as 'McKartane'. In 1335 AD, King Edward III ordered £10 to be paid to Henry deMandeville for his skirmishes with the Chief Macartan, who allegedly attempted to plunder the manor of the Norman Lord, Roger Outlawe, Prior of Kilmanham. He had at least one son:

    i)   **Tomas Mor macSean Macartán** (*Thomas Curtin*),
                (*See Generation 16 below*)

[6] J.W. Hanna, 'Clough', Down Recorder, 11August 1861
[7] TCD - Calendar Close Rolls 1333/37
[8] O' Laverty Rev James, History of the Diocese of Down and Connor, Davidson, vol1 p83

16)   Tomás Mor macSean Macartán

(Thomas the Great Curtin)

son of Sean son Donnchad of son of Giolla Colm son of Cinnait son of Eochaid son of Domnall son of Giolla Colm son of Ciannait son of Raghnall son of Searran son of Eochaidh son of Concruach MacArtán, son of Crum na-Cruach MacArtán, son of Cuonincon MacArtán, son of Artán

Chief of the Macartan Clan, King of Cíneal Fógartaígh

He must have been born about 1285, Chief of the Macartan clan, Lord of Uíbh Eatách. His first mentioned in 1343 AD as ambushing Sir Ralph D'Ufford, the royal Judiciar of Ireland upon his arrival at the pass of Emmerdullah. The Lord Judiciar lost his clothing, money, vessels of silver and some horses. It was only with the assistance of tribal allied in Co. Louth that he was able to enter the country. In the spring of 1345 AD, D'Ufford again attempted to enter Ulster with an army of conscripts. He attempted to enter through the Moyra pass, where he was confronted by Thomas and his armed clansmen. He was initially setback by the local resistance, however he eventually took the upper hand, defeating Thomas in battle and banishing him from the king's lands. Moreover, to ensure that he declared Thomas an outlaw, offering a reward for his capture, stating that he was "an Irishman giving himself the name of King of Ovegh, alive or dead. In 1347, Thomas was again defeated in battle, was taken prisoner by the English garrison and hanged the Banbrigde. Subsequent to his death, no Macartan chief was powerful enough to claim the title of king. All subsequent claimants occupied the role of vassals under the Magennis kings. The deeds of Thomas were famous that his later French descendants in the 19th century would recount his military exploits against the forces of the English crown. Hereafter, they continue as sub-chieftains under the more powerful Macgennis kings[9].

The death of Thomas Mor was recounted by various bards in the latter half of the 14th century, as the Gaelic chieftains were slowly overcome by Anglo-Norman military prowess and technology. Their generosity to the bardic class, the Ollams, appears to be remembered and admired by the Gaelic scholars of that epoch. John O'Dugan, the Chief Poet of the O'Kelly clan said this about the clan Macartan:

> *Macartan has by charter*
> *The steady stout Cinel-Faghartaigh*
> *Who never refuse gifts to the clergy*
> *They are the treasury of hospitality.*

Conversely, later Elizabethian poets appear to express an alternative opinion regarding the constitutions and moral center of the Macartans. Aenghus O'Daly

> *The Cinel-Faghartaigh are the men!*
> *Remnants of curses and lies,*
> *Large, soft, dastardly men,*
> *Blind crocked shin-burnt.*

Later references to his life seem to be apocryphal, as he appears to take on the trappings of the ancient druid class- levitating, travelling exceedingly long distances overnight, and soothsaying. He is granted the post-nomen 'na-Faidh' in some incidences, meaning 'the prophet'. If he had any writing, they do not appear to survive until the present in his hand. Of his predictions, he lays claim that a "star will arise out of the house of Macartan". Either Tomas' exploits or this prediction must have been famous, as his later French descendants recount his life well into the 19th century. His wife was an unnamed woman of the Magenis clan, with her he had at least one son:

    i)   **Tomás Oge macTomas Macartán**, (*See Generation 17 below*)

    ii)   **Donnchad macTomas Macartán,**

    iii)   **Caitlin ingenTomas Macartán**, allegedly married a Norman knight by the name deCharnei.

---

[9] Simms, K, The Gaelic Lordship of Ulster, Ph.D. thesis, TCD, 1976

17) Tomás Oge macTomás Mor Macartán

(Thomas the Younger Curtin)

son of Tomas Mor son of Sean son of Donnchad of son of Giolla Colm son of Cinnait son of Eochaid son of Domnall son of Giolla Colm son of Ciannait son of Raghnall son of Searran son of Eochaidh son of Concruach MacArtán, son of Crum na-Cruach MacArtán, son of Cuonincon MacArtán, son of Artán

He must have been born around the year 1310 AD. Dubhaltach MacFirbisigh gives him the post-nomen 'Peampaidite', which appears in no other annalist. It's meaning is unknown, but it might relate to his father's clairvoyant abilities. Nothing else is known about his life. He had at least one son:

   i)   **Searran macTomas**, *(See Generation 18 below)*

   ii)   **Rohesia ingenTomas**, who married James Russel, 3rd Baron of Killough in 1370 AD. This is an English name, the Irish equivalent must have been 'Róisín'. She was the mother of George Russell, 4th Baron of Killough, and the subsequent House of Russell which endures to this day.

---

18) Searran macTomás Oge Macartán

son of Tomas Oge son of Tomas Mor son of Sean son of Donnchad of son of Giolla Colm son of Cinnait son of Eochaid son of Domnall son of Giolla Colm son of Ciannait son of Raghnall son of Searran son of Eochaidh son of Concruach MacArtán, son of Crum na-Cruach MacArtán, son of Cuonincon MacArtán, son of Artán

He was born about 1335 AD. Nothing else is known about his life. The repetition of his name with his ancestor has caused various scribal errors. He had at least one son:

   i)   **Giolla Padraig macSearran**, *(See Generation 19 below)*

---

19)   Giolla Padraig macSearran Macartán

(Gilpatrick Curtin)

son of Searran son of Tomas Oge son of Tomas Mor son of Sean son of Donnchad of son of Giolla Colm son of Cinnait son of Eochaid son of Domnall son of Giolla Colm son of Ciannait son of Raghnall son of Searran son of Eochaidh son of Concruach MacArtán, son of Crum na-Cruach MacArtán, son of Cuonincon MacArtán, son of Artán

He was born about 1360 AD. Nothing else is known about his life. He had at least one son:

    i)   **Giolla Domnall macGiolla Padraig**, *(See Generation 20 below)*
    ii)   **Giolla Padraig Oge,**
    iii) **Giolla Domnaig,**

---

20)   Giolla Domnall macGiolla Padraig Macartán

(Gildaniel Curtin)

son of Giolla Padraig son of Searran son of Tomas Oge son of Tomas Mor son of Sean son of Donnchad of son of Giolla Colm son of Cinnait son of Eochaid son of Domnall son of Giolla Colm son of Ciannait son of Raghnall son of Searran son of Eochaidh son of Concruach MacArtán, son of Crum na-Cruach MacArtán, son of Cuonincon MacArtán, son of Artán

He was born about 1385 AD. Nothing else is known about his life. He had at least one son:

    i)   **Giolla Droigin macGiolla Domnall**, *(See Generation 21 below)*

---

21)   Giolla Droigin macGiolla Domnall Macartán

(Gildroigin Curtin)

son of Giolla Domnall son of Giolla Padraig son of Searran son of Tomas Oge son of Tomas Mor son of Sean son of Donnchad of son of Giolla Colm son of Cinnait son of Eochaid son of Domnall son of Giolla Colm son of Ciannait son of Raghnall son of Searran son of Eochaidh son of Concruach MacArtán, son of Crum na-Cruach MacArtán, son of Cuonincon MacArtán, son of Artán

He was born about 1410 AD. Nothing else is known about his life. He had at least one son:

    i)   **Giolla Colm macGiolla Droigin**, *(See Generation 22 below)*

22) Giolla Colm macGiolla Droigin Macartán

(Gilcolumba Curtin)

son of Giolla Colm son of Giolla Domnall son of Giolla Padraig son of Searran son of Tomas Oge son of Tomas Mor son of Sean son of Donnchad of son of Giolla Colm son of Cinnait son of Eochaid son of Domnall son of Giolla Colm son of Ciannait son of Raghnall son of Searran son of Eochaidh son of Concruach MacArtán, son of Crum na-Cruach MacArtán, son of Cuonincon MacArtán, son of Artán

He was born about 1435 AD. His mother was allegedly a Scottish woman. Nothing else is known about his life. He had at least one son:

     i)   **Eachmilidh macGiolla Colm**, *(See Generation 23 below)*

---

23) Eachmilidh macGiolla Colm Macartán

(Emilius Curtin)

son of Giolla Colm son of Giolla Droigin son of Giolla Domnall son of Giolla Padraig son of Searran son of Tomas Oge son of Tomas Mor son of Sean son of Donnchad of son of Giolla Colm son of Cinnait son of Eochaid son of Domnall son of Giolla Colm son of Ciannait son of Raghnall son of Searran son of Eochaidh son of Concruach MacArtán, son of Crum na-Cruach MacArtán, son of Cuonincon MacArtán, son of Artán

He was born about 1460 AD. This name is also used heavily by the MacGuiness clan, which might presuppose some intermarriage the generation prior. However, women are rarely noted in these records, and historical record of Irish marriages in the medieval period are almost non-existant. Nothing else is known about his life. Again, the repetition of names appears to have confused later chroniclers, who appear to confuse his place in the genealogy with his 16th century descendent of the same name. He had at least one son:

     i)   **Aedh macEachmilidh**, *(Hugh Curtin) (See Generation 24 below)*

Henry VII, Lord of Ireland 1485-1509

24)   Aedh macEachmilidh Macartán

(Hugh Curtin)

son of Eachmilidh son of Giolla Colm son of Giolla Droigin son of Giolla Domnall son of Giolla Padraig son of Searran son of Tomas Oge son of Tomas Mor son of Sean son of Donnchad of son of Giolla Colm son of Cinnait son of Eochaid son of Domnall son of Giolla Colm son of Ciannait son of Raghnall son of Searran son of Eochaidh son of Concruach MacArtán, son of Crum na-Cruach MacArtán, son of Cuonincon MacArtán, son of Artán

He appears to be the "Hugh Roe" Macartan mentioned in the annals, not to be confused with the Hugh Roe O'Neill who was a contemporary. His limited involvement in national affairs would have been to limit the expansion of Tudor power in Ireland during the late 15th century. He had at least one son:

    i)   **Turlogh macAedh**, *(Charles Curtin) (See Generation 25 below)*

    ii)   **Patrick macAedh,** *(Patrick Curtin)*, died in 1493. It is not clear why his passing is noted in the local annals.

25) Turlogh macAedh Macartán

(Charles Curtin)

son of Aedh son of Eachmilidh son of Giolla Colm son of Giolla Droigin son of Giolla Domnall son of Giolla Padraig son of Searran son of Tomas Oge son of Tomas Mor son of Sean son of Donnchad of son of Giolla Colm son of Cinnait son of Eochaid son of Domnall son of Giolla Colm son of Ciannait son of Raghnall son of Searran son of Eochaidh son of Concruach MacArtán, son of Crum na-Cruach MacArtán, son of Cuonincon MacArtán, son of Artán

He was born about 1510 AD, and perhaps died during the reign of Elizabeth I or Mary I. His lifetime saw the English reconquest of Ireland and the spark of the Protestant Reformation. Since Ulster was largely backwater, and Ireland had no university, it is unlikely that he would have been aware of the tumult developing on the continent in the early 16th century. Nothing else is known about his life. He had at least one son:

> i) **Phelim macTurlogh**, *(Philomen Curtin)* *(See Generation 26 below)*

121)   Phelim macTurlogh Macartán

(Philomen Curtin)

son of Turlogh son of Aedh son of Eachmilidh son of Giolla Colm son of Giolla Droigin son of Giolla Domnall son of Giolla Padraig son of Searran son of Tomas Oge son of Tomas Mor son of Sean son of Donnchad of son of Giolla Colm son of Cinnait son of Eochaid son of Domnall son of Giolla Colm son of Ciannait son of Raghnall son of Searran son of Eochaidh son of Concruach MacArtán, son of Crum na-Cruach MacArtán, son of Cuonincon MacArtán, son of Artán

He was born about 1535 AD. He must have died before 1584, as his son was regarded as the head of the clan. Nothing else is known about his life. He had at least one son:

    ii)   **Eachmilidh macPhelim**, *(Emilius Curtin)* *(See Generation 27 below)*

27) Eachmilidh macPhelim Macartán

(Emilius Curtin)

son of Phelim son of Aedh son of Eachmilidh son of Giolla Colm son of Giolla Droigin son of Giolla Domnall son of Giolla Padraig son of Searran son of Tomas Oge son of Tomas Mor son of Sean son of Donnchad of son of Giolla Colm son of Cinnait son of Eochaid son of Domnall son of Giolla Colm son of Ciannait son of Raghnall son of Searran son of Eochaidh son of Concruach MacArtán, son of Crum na-Cruach MacArtán, son of Cuonincon MacArtán, son of Artán

Chief of the Clan Macartan, Lord of Kinelarty

He was born about 1560 AD. He is first mentioned in 1575 AD as being suspected of treason by Sir Henry Sydney, where he is called "Acholie mcCartan". The following year he appears before the Lord Deputy of Ireland, Sir John Perrot, along with the other chiefs of Ulster to swear fidelity to the English crown. At this time, he was required to give hostages and assist in conscriptions from his own land holdings. In a note dated October 7th, 1584 AD and indenture was made between this same Lord Deputy, the royal council and "Acholie MacCartan" regarding obtaining footmen from his demesne. The Macartan chief appears to be in good standing with the crown at this time. However, this appears to be short-lived, as he joined with Sorley Boy McDonnell to attack Lower Claneboy the following year. It is not until the outbreak of the Nine-Year wat that we see the overt rebellion of the Macartan clan. In a letter of April 5th 1584, Hugh O'Neills to the Earl of Kildare, he notes that the Macartan chieftain has yet to come an join the rebellion against the English crown. The following year, 1585 AD, we see that the Macartan clan has joined the rebellion and declared fealty to O'Neill to resist the forces of the English crown. Queen Elizabeth and her deputies attained Acholie Macartan, claiming that he continued to practice tanistry, and that his lands were forfeited to the crown for his sedition. Nothing else is known about his life. He had at least one son:

    i)   **Phelim macEachmilidh**, *(Philomen Curtin)* *(See Generation 28a below)*

    ii)   **Antóin macEachmilidh**, *(Anthony Curtin)*

    iii)   **Padraig macEachmilidh**, *(Patrick Curtin)*

    iv)   **Eogan macEachmilidh**, *(Owen Curtin)* *(See Generation 28b below)*

    v)   **Donnchad Oge macEachmilidh**, *(Donoagh Curtin)* who is only mentioned at the death of Lord Cromwell in 1607. His later whereabouts are unclear.

English Settler of the Elizabethan Plantation, circa 1600

28a) Phelim macEachmilidh Macartán

(Philomen Curtin)

son of Eachmilidh son of Phelim son of Turlogh son of Aedh son of Eachmilidh son of Giolla Colm son of Giolla Droigin son of Giolla Domnall son of Giolla Padraig son of Searran son of Tomas Oge son of Tomas Mor son of Sean son of Donnchad of son of Giolla Colm son of Cinnait son of Eochaid son of Domnall son of Giolla Colm son of Ciannait son of Raghnall son of Searran son of Eochaidh son of Concruach MacArtán, son of Crum na-Cruach MacArtán, son of Cuonincon MacArtán, son of Artán

Chief of the Clan Macartan, Lord of Kinelarty

Born: around 1585, Co. Down, Kingdom of Ireland
Died: June 10th 1631, Drumaroad, Co. Down, Kingdom of Ireland

The exact timeframe for when he took the chieftainship of proprietorship of Kinelarty is unclear. His father, Eachmilidh, may have been removed from office as a result of support of Hugh O'Neill, although this is uncertain. Eachmilidh was noted as being "captain" over the region as late as 1608. His first known act as chieftain is also his most infamous. On September 28th, 1605, he relinquished ownership of one third of the lands of Kinelarty to Edward Cromwell, 3rd Baron Cromwell. Cromwell would die two years later on September 12th, 1607 and this estate was purchased by Matthew Forde for the sum of eight thousand pounds. This act was ultimately an act of betrayal on the part of Phelim, as the territory of the Macartan was owned by the clan and not an individual chieftain. Therefore, the sale of this property was perceived as a violation of the chieftain's own purview and their duty to *noblesse oblige.* As part of this land deal with Lord Cromwell, it was written that Patrick Macartan would be educated and brought up 'in a manner fitting a gentleman'. He apparently was able to maintain the loyalty of some of his own clan, as in 1608 he is still in charge of sixty men at arms.

The Macartans appear to have been subjected to regular forfeiture at this time, as the crown assumed proprietorship of some of their lands in CO. Kerry and granted them to Thomas Fitzmaurice, 18th Lord of Linax in 1612. In 1615 in retaliation for this Phelim is reputed to have raided the Burgesses of Ardglass, where there was an armed skirmish. Following this, and perhaps as a result of this, part of the Macartan lands were taken and assigned to Sir Francis Annesley in 1617. He appears to have survived well into the 1630's, as he is mentioned in a state inquisition of 1634. The final record of his life is his own initials 'PMC' which he engraved above the doorway of McCartan's chapel in Loughinisland about 1636. Some assign the date of June 1631 as the date of his death, but this is chronologically impossible for the aforementioned reasons. The exact date of his death is unknown.

He appears to have married a Magennis, daughter of Hugh Viscount Iveagh, and had at least three sons:

i) **Padraig macPhelim**, (*Patrick Curtin*) (*See Generation 29a below*)

ii) **Ogan macPhelim**, (*Owen Curtin*), who is said to have visited Owen Roe O'Neill several times at Charlemont fort during the Confederate Wars.

iii) **Domnall Oge macPhelim,** (*Daniel Curtin*) He is mentioned releasing his right to properties in Kinelarty along with his father. It might be assumed that he is the eldest son for this reason.

iv) **Aileanóra ingenPhelim,** (*Elinor Curtin*) who married Matthew Forde in 1621. He was the clerk of Nisi Prius the Commissioners of Ulster. He purchased Coolgreany estate sometime before 1637. He became a member of Irish Parliament in 164a AD. They had four children: Katherine Forde (1626), Ann Forde (1636), Henry Forde (1639) and Nicholas Forde. Nicholas was the only child who appears to have survived into adulthood. He would go on to marry, Elizabeth Loftus, daughter of Sir Adam Loftus.

28b) Eogan macEachmilidh Macartán

(John Curtin)

son of Eachmilidh son of Phelim son of Turlogh son of Aedh son of Eachmilidh son of Giolla Colm son of Giolla Droigin son of Giolla Domnall son of Giolla Padraig son of Searran son of Tomas Oge son of Tomas Mor son of Sean son of Donnchad of son of Giolla Colm son of Cinnait son of Eochaid son of Domnall son of Giolla Colm son of Ciannait son of Raghnall son of Searran son of Eochaidh son of Concruach MacArtán, son of Crum na-Cruach MacArtán, son of Cuonincon MacArtán, son of Artán

The Gaelic name he is given- "Eogan" is curious, as it does not appear as a common name of the period. It appears to be transliterated most commonly as 'Owen', as such is the case with latter members of the family with this name. For reasons that are unclear Owen is not mentioned by O'Hart in his Irish pedigree of the Macartan clan, naming only three sons of Eachmilidh. He appears only in the genealogy of Fr. Cornelius Curtain, a century of this. It is likely that he is the same as the "Owen McCartan", who was pardoned by the crown in 1584 AD, with the caveat that such a pardon was "not to include any offences in the reign of the present deputy". He appears to have been invested in the military exploits of the Nine-Year war and engaged in the disastrous campaign in Munster, ultimately culminating in the Battle of Kinsale in October of 1601 AD. There he was taken as hostage, along with other members of the Macartan clan by George Carew, Lord-President of Munster. It is unclear what directly followed this period, but it seems likely that he would have been employed as a bondsmen or awaited trial for sedition against the crown. In either case, no formal charges against Owen were retained, and all Irish rebels were granted a universal pardon by King James I in 1604 in an attempt to subdue some of the tumultuousness of the region. Moreover, he appears to have been pardoned again in 1609, along with a large number of his clansmen. Following these pardons, he appears to have remained in Munster, although in what capacity is uncertain. In 1605, his brother Phelim would sell the clan-lands around Kinelarty to Lord Cromwell. Consequently, no native Irish were permitted to settle the land, as by royal edict it was only open to English and Scottish settlers. His wife is not found in any record, but he had at least two sons:

 i) **Giolla Padraig macEogan**, *(GilPatrick Curtin)* *(See Generation 29b below)*

 ii) **Domnall macEogan**, *(Daniel Curtin)* *(See Generation 129c below)*

The entry of the Macartans into Munster and into County Cork and Kerry in particular is an event that is difficult to fully identity. Prior to the year 1500 there appears to be no 'Curtins' or any variant of that last name residing in either county. The MacCruithins, who were indigenous to County Clare, could be found in Limerick, but no further. How and where the abundances of Curtins derived from is unclear.

registered in that year. Ó Corbáin had in one of his poems derived the young priest's family from Eibhear, the reputed ancestor of the principal families of Munster. David denied this, and held that the Mac Cartáins of Munster were of the same race as the Mac Cartáins of Ulster, and consequently were descended from Ir, son of Míle Easpáinne. Accordingly, he sent the correct genealogy of the head of the Mac Cartáins of Ulster to the priest, accompanied by the following note:—

"Rev⁴. Fath⁴.,

"Because I see by Poet Corban's ingenious Poems that he is better versed in the Old Testament and other Foreign Transactions than in the Ancient Histories of Ireland, whereas he Derives your Pedigree from Heber, the Stock from whom the Noble Families of Munster are Descended, whereas your Family are Descended Linally and Originally from Ire mac Miles, the Stock of the Nobility of Ulster, I here send you the Genealogy of the Head of your Family and consequently of yourself."

We find that the Macartans had landholdings in Kerry in the late 16th century, and that they had a number of refuges take asylum with the Earl of Desmond at this time. The decimation of County Down make this expedient, as there was no means of carving out an agrarian existence in that border country. However, even this influx of immigration would not constitute the vast number of 'Curtins' residing in Co. Cork or why this is a scarcity of records. Even the earliest Anglo-Irish historians appear to be confused on the subject. Perhaps this is why O'Harts pedigree does not mention any Curtins of Cork specifically.

It seems that the most likely solution to this issue is that the Curtins of Cork and Kerry are descendants of both a MacCruthin diaspora throughout Munster, as well as the refugees of the clan Macartan. This can be further understood through the person of Fr. Cornelius Curtain, a man of Macartan descent, who eventually adopted the Munster spelling of the surname, despite not having any ancestral connection to the MacCrutihins of Clare. Therefore, it might be safe to assume that Fr. Curtain was the rule rather than the exception, and that all Macartans who entered Munster followed suit, adapting their name to fit the paradigm of Dalcassian tribes. This is at least partially an *argumentum ex silento*, as there is no documentation to make this certain. However, this cannot be fully surprising, as there was never a standardization of Gaelic spelling in Celtic Ireland (such an institution would not appear until the 20th century). Moreover, it would be peculiar that such records could be maintained amidst the tumult of Ireland in the 17th century.

From a 1641 deposition of alleged atrocities committed by the Irish against colonists of the crown

29a) Patrick Macartan

(Giolla Padraig macPhelim Macartan)

son of Phelim son of Eachmilidh son of Phelim son of Turlogh son of Aedh son of Eachmilidh son of Giolla Colm son of Giolla Droigin son of Giolla Domnall son of Giolla Padraig son of Searran son of Tomas Oge son of Tomas Mor son of Sean son of Donnchad of son of Giolla Colm son of Cinnait son of Eochaid son of Domnall son of Giolla Colm son of Ciannait son of Raghnall son of Searran son of Eochaidh son of Concruach MacArtán, son of Crum na-Cruach MacArtán, son of Cuonincon MacArtán, son of Artán

Lord of Kinelarty, Chief of the Macartans

Born: abt. 1591, Ballydromroe, Co. Down, Kingdom of Ireland

Died: 1642, Co. Down, Kingdom of Ireland

Married: Cecilia O'Berne

He is mentioned in the pedigree as given by O'Hart. According to the terms of the deal conducted by his father, Phelim, Chief of the Name, Patrick was to be brought up and educated in the manner benefiting an English gentleman. This task would have fallen to his son and heir, Thomas Cromwell, 1st Earl of Ardglass. Given that Ireland had only one university present in the 17th century, he would have had some connection to Trinity College in Dublin. However, no public record of Patrick's time there can be found. Little is noted of his life until the outbreak of war in 1641. The political tension that was building up over the course of his lifetime would have hit fever pitch as Ireland revolted against King Charles I, and began attacking the Anglo-Irish lord, their colonists and agents, and begin destroying the hated 'Church of Ireland', which they were forced to be tithed under. Patrick must have been involved in the rebellion early on, as Dublin Castle issues £300 reward for his head. This act of sedition was a significant gamble, as the previous attempt to drive the English out a generation prior resulted in the decimation of Kinelarty and the attainted status of some of his familial lands. Shortly thereafter he is noted as meeting with Owen O'Neill, sending him as envoy to the King of France for potential military assistance against the English. Unsurprisingly, his home in Anadoorn, the traditional residence of the Lord of Kinelarty was burned by Colonel Chichester in 1642 as well. He was travelling with the infantry corps along with Rory McGuire, the McMahons, McGennises and O'Cahans. It seems likely that he was the other McCartan leader noted as being killed at the Battle of Kilwarlin Wood in April of 1642 against the Scottish and English armies. The report of 'Owen and Patrick Macartan' being captured likely applies to his children and not to Patrick himself.

Children of PATRICK MACARTAN and CECILIA O'BERNE are:

i) **John Macartan**, (Eogan Macartan) (*See generation 30a below*)

ii) **Patrick Macartan**, (Giolla Padraig Macartan)

Sir Richard Boyle (1566-1643), 1st Earl of Cork 1620-1643, Lord-Treasurer of the Kingdom of Ireland

29c) Domnall MacCurtain,

(Daniel Curtane)

son of Eogan son of Eachmilidh son of Phelim son of Turlogh son of Aedh son of Eachmilidh son of Giolla Colm son of Giolla Droigin son of Giolla Domnall son of Giolla Padraig son of Searran son of Tomas Oge son of Tomas Mor son of Sean son of Donnchad of son of Giolla Colm son of Cinnait son of Eochaid son of Domnall son of Giolla Colm son of Ciannait son of Raghnall son of Searran son of Eochaidh son of Concruach MacArtán, son of Crum na-Cruach MacArtán, son of Cuonincon MacArtán, son of Artán

Also references as 'Daniel MacCurtain', or 'Daniel Curtane'. He appears to be the primary estate holder for the MacCurtain family in the early 17th century and may have been the elder son. The majority of information that survives regarding his life is taken from the memoirs of Richard Boyle, 1st Earl of Cork, whom Domnall had financial dealing with throughout in the 1620's. It appears that a large loan and tracts of land were leased to this for several years late in the reign of King James I. This relationship appears to be copasetic prior to the Confederate wars, and no issues between Domnall and the Earl appear to have been noted in his remembrance. Domnall appears to have brought him own family further into the Anglosphere, as two of his sons are stated in the context of the Earl of Cork. This is not entirely surprising as the Earl's bitter legacy in Cork is tied to that of English colonialism. During the zenith of his power, his municipal expansion employed over four thousand natives in his administration, largely in the rebellious North of Cork. Domnall and his children appear to have been tied to the developing colonial government. However, Domnall's fate and that of his children have been lost to time. They likely disappeared into the fabric of Irish society following the Cromwellian invasion and the destruction of the former Gaelic order.

> 17 *Oct.*, 1625.
> Edmond Farish and Morish Gold, Petty Serjeants.
> Edmond Barret, Gunner and Yeoman to the Mayor.
> Nicholas Verdon and John Dahill, under Porters.
> James Curtane, Drummer.
> George Wise and Dom^s. White, Yeomen for the Sheriffs.
> Edmond Mortymer, Bellman.

Domnall's wife is not noted in any source, but at least two sons are noted in the surviving historical records:

i. **James Curtane**, (*Seamus MacCartan*) he is stated as being a dummer in the retinue of the Earl, working in Cork City proper between 1614 and 1625. There do not appear to be any other family members residing in the city at that time, and the rendering of his name as 'Curtane' is curious, as it is intentionally anglicized. The name 'James' does not appear amongst any ancestor. It might be taken from his wife's family, or alternatively, as a tribute to the reign of King James VI & I.

ii. **John Curtane**, (*Sean MacCartan*) his early life is unknown. John is said to have attended the University of Oxford, studying "physicks and alchemical science". This record survives from the school providentially, as he was permanently expelled in 1648 for reasons that have been lost to history. The date of '1648' is suspicious, as this was the year of the execution of King Charles I, and it could be speculated that John held sympathies to the House of Stuart. His connection to Robert Boyle, father of Modern Chemistry is possible, but speculative. Currently, there is no documentation linking their respective careers known at this time.

Johes Curtane for that it was made appeare that hee was put in by the Visitors unduely in the the yeare of our Lord 1648 and for that hee studyeth or professeth Physick contrary to the Coll· Statutes   This board decreede him to bee removed out of his said fellowship   And did then remove him. And did farther order that all the profitts and emoluments of his said fellowship be sequestered and continue sequestered to the said Coll use in the hands of the Rector and Scholars there untill such tyme that all debts by him owing to the said Coll and all damages by him done bee fully discharged and satisfied

Ordered by this Board that a decree bee sent forth, for him the said Mr Hitchcock to voyde his chambers within fower dayes.

Droghedah so bloked up that a bushell of wheate was sold for 23 shill., & meate scarce to be had at any rate. Jan. 4 1641

Drogheda

30a) John Macartan

(Eogan macGiolla Padraig Macartan)

son of Giolla Padraig son of Phelim son of Eachmilidh son of Phelim son of Turlogh son of Aedh son of Eachmilidh son of Giolla Colm son of Giolla Droigin son of Giolla Domnall son of Giolla Padraig son of Searran son of Tomas Oge son of Tomas Mor son of Sean son of Donnchad of son of Giolla Colm son of Cinnait son of Eochaid son of Domnall son of Giolla Colm son of Ciannait son of Raghnall son of Searran son of Eochaidh son of Concruach MacArtán, son of Crum na-Cruach MacArtán, son of Cuonincon MacArtán, son of Artán

Chief of the Clan Macartan

Born: abt. 1640, Ballydromerode, Co. Down, Kingdom of Ireland
Died: Sept. 26, 1736, Co. Down, Kingdom of Ireland
Married: Bridget Luck Forde (also spelled 'Brigette'), born in Coolgreeney, Co. Wexford, Kingdom of Ireland. Her parentage is unknown.

John Macartan's early life is unrecorded in any Irish Annals, and no family records seem to survive the tumultuous 17th century. His father had been killed in his childhood, so he must have been raised by his mother's family, the Forde's. John appears to have been present at the Battle of the Boyne in 1690, although he does not appear to e in the official register of the Irish Army. Subsequent to this defeat, he fled Ireland for France, where he became a captain in the Irish Brigade of the French Royal Army. The Jacobite Peerage appointed John Macartan as a Commissioner for County Down, in an attempt to raise funds for the purposes of opposing King William III and his opposition army. Most of his lands were attainted and he was not fully restored to his former status. His return to Ireland is unspecified, although it must have happened sometime before his death, as he was buried at Macartan's Chapel in Loughinisland. However, his descendants appear to have gained a footing in French society and appear to rise through the rank of the native aristocracy through the 18th and 19th centuries.

Children of JOHN MACARTAN and BRIDGET FORDE are:

i) **Anthony Joseph Macartan**, (Antóin Seosamh Macartan) (*See generation 31a below*)

ii) **Phelim Macartan**, He assumed the head of the family after the expulsion of his father to France by the English Army. Phelim died in 1751 and was buried in the churchyard in Loughlinisland. The name of his wife is unknown and does not survive in any record. He was the father of Dominick Macartan, who married Ann O'Niell in 1766. They had two sons and three daughters. In their life they were known to give heavily to the Franciscan Friars in County Down. Phelim died March 1772, at the age of 78. He is buried in Loughlinisland graveyard. Both Phelim and Dominick were regarded the last chiefs of the name at the time of their respective deaths. However, following this no genealogy appears to survive. Moreover, the land holdings of the Macartans of County Down evaporate following a long land dispute with an English landlord in 1768.

iii) **Patrick Macartan**, of him nothing is known or recorded. It is likely that he died in infancy.

Irish Soldiers in the service of the French Crown, 18th century

31a) Anthony Joseph Macartan

(Antóin Seosamh Macartan)

son of Eogan son of Giolla Padraig son of Phelim son of Eachmilidh son of Phelim son of Turlogh son of Aedh son of Eachmilidh son of Giolla Colm son of Giolla Droigin son of Giolla Domnall son of Giolla Padraig son of Searran son of Tomas Oge son of Tomas Mor son of Sean son of Donnchad of son of Giolla Colm son of Cinnait son of Eochaid son of Domnall son of Giolla Colm son of Ciannait son of Raghnall son of Searran son of Eochaidh son of Concruach MacArtán, son of Crum na-Cruach MacArtán, son of Cuonincon MacArtán, son of Artán

Born: about 1680, Co. Down, Kingdom of Ireland
Died: May 6, 1758, Montreuil-sur-Mer, Pas de Calais, Kingdom of France
Married: 1st wife- Suzanne de Cologon, at Saint-Catherine of Lille on May 7, 1736; 2nd wife- Marie Catherine Hayez
Occupation: Army Captain in the Irish Brigade of the French Royal Army

Children of ANTHONY MACARTAN and MARIE HAYEZ are:
i)   **Anthony Joseph Macartan**, (Antóin Seosamh Macartan) (*See generation 32a below*)

32a) Anthony Joseph Macartan

(Antóin Seosamh Macartan)

son of Antóin son of Eogan son of Giolla Padraig son of Phelim son of Eachmilidh son of Phelim son of Turlogh son of Aedh son of Eachmilidh son of Giolla Colm son of Giolla Droigin son of Giolla Domnall son of Giolla Padraig son of Searran son of Tomas Oge son of Tomas Mor son of Sean son of Donnchad of son of Giolla Colm son of Cinnait son of Eochaid son of Domnall son of Giolla Colm son of Ciannait son of Raghnall son of Searran son of Eochaidh son of Concruach MacArtán, son of Crum na-Cruach MacArtán, son of Cuonincon MacArtán, son of Artán

Born: about 1716
Baptized: (unknown), perhaps in France
Married: Anne Joseph Felicite Piette, on January 8, 1753, Valenciennes, Flandre, Kingdom of France.
Died: Sept. 6, 1787, Hauts-de-France, Kingdom of France

Children of ANTHONY JOSEPH MACARTAN and ANNE JOSEPH FELICITE PIETTE are:

i) **Andronique Xavier Isidore Macartan**, (Aidrean Sabhair Ahdhori Macartan). Born on Sept. 21, 1764 in Paroisse saint-Jacques, Valenciennes, Hauts-de-France, Kingdom of France. He married Françoise Anne Fleming, probably in London, as they fled from the revolution. They had one daughter, Marie Angélique Macartan, who married Henri Louis Alphonse Joseph Delannoy, also in London following the demise of Napoleon. She is the direct ancestor of French President Charles deGaulle, who claims Irish descent through this ancestor.

ii) **Marie Angélique Macartan**, she married a French gentleman of the surname of Momal, but little is known of her life. Her son, Jacques Francois Momal, is mentioned as being present at the death of her father.

iii) **Mathurin Louis Joseph Macartan,** (Máirtín Lugh Seosamh Macartan) Born Aug. 25, 1770 in Valenciennes saint-Jacques, Kingdom of France. His later fate is unknown. More likely than not he was killed during the inflammation of the French Revolution.

CHAPTER II

Establishment of the
MacCurtains of County Cork

1603 AD through 1798 AD

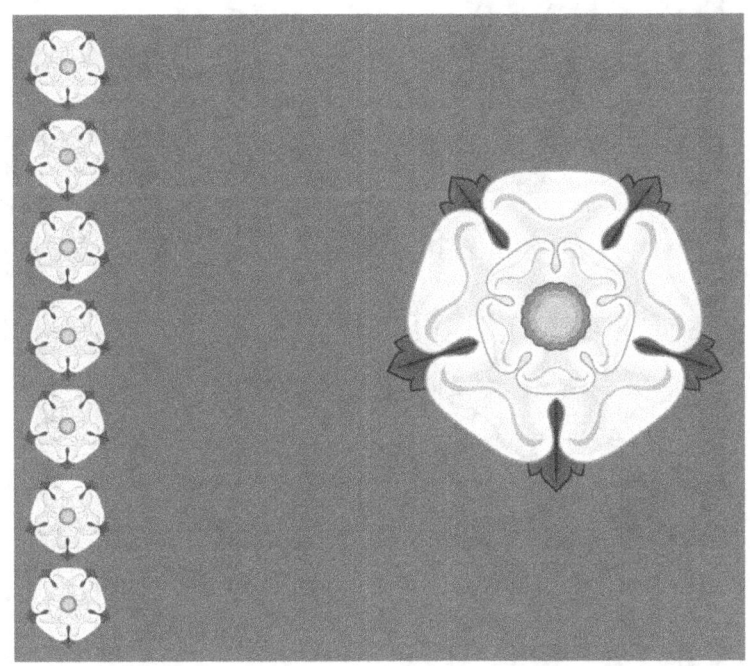

Article I:
'Audentior Ibo'
(*I shall go more boldly*)

Captain Cornelius Curtain: his ancestors and progeny
1685-1870

James VI & I Stuart, King of Scotland, England and Ireland

29b) GiollaPadraig MacCurtain

(Gilpatrick Curtin)

son of Eogan son of Eachmilidh son of Phelim son of Turlogh son of Aedh son of Eachmilidh son of Giolla Colm son of Giolla Droigin son of Giolla Domnall son of Giolla Padraig son of Searran son of Tomas Oge son of Tomas Mor son of Sean son of Donnchad of son of Giolla Colm son of Cinnait son of Eochaid son of Domnall son of Giolla Colm son of Ciannait son of Raghnall son of Searran son of Eochaidh son of Concruach MacArtán, son of Crum na-Cruach MacArtán, son of Cuonincon MacArtán, son of Artán

The nativity and early life of GiollaPadraig are obscured by the destitute state that his father, Eogan, experienced following the Battle of Kinsale. He appears to have resided in northern County Cork. His uncle Phellim had sold off the familial estates in County Down, which were heavily depopulated in the wake of the Nine-Year War. He appears to have married an O'Sullivan, the heiress of an estate near Mallow. Given that his son was noted as the proprietor of the estate in Cromwellian times, he likely died during or before the Confederate Wars.

i. **Phellim MacCurtain**, (*See Generation 30b*)

ii. **Conchobhar MacCurtain**, [*Also known as Fr. Cornelius Curtain*], (*See Generation 30c*).

iii. **(daughter),** who married an unknown Spanish soldier

30b)   Phellim MacCurtain

(Philomen Curtin)

son of GiollaPadraig son of Eogan son of Eachmilidh son of Phelim son of Turlogh son of Aedh son of Eachmilidh of Giolla Colm son of Giolla Droigin son of Giolla Domnall son of Giolla Padraig son of Searran son of Tomas Oge son of Tomas Mor son of Sean son of Donnchad of son of Giolla Colm son of Cinnait son of Eochaid son of Domnall son of Giolla Colm son of Ciannait son of Raghnall son of Searran son of Eochaidh son of Concruach MacArtán, son of Crum na-Cruach MacArtán, son of Cuonincon MacArtán, son of Artán

He is perhaps the first Curtin to step onto the pages of history with any contemporary clarity. His birth must have been between 1625 and 1635, likely in the Mallow farmlands held by the MacCurtain family. Across English records he is given the name Phelim [or Phellim] Curtane. This anglicization might presumed to only exist in English records, although this cannot be substantiated. Since there are no surviving Gaelic accounts it is not clear whether this anglicization of the surname was intentional or not. It does appear that the Curtain family maintained strong national ties between 1605 and 1640, as they appear to straddle the line between the English administration and the Gaelic gentry.

He is noted on a list of King Charles I's royal Irish army granted the officer's title of ensign. Little is given historically of his military career, with the exception of its conclusion. He is noted as being present at the siege of Drogheda in late 1649, wherein he was taken capture along with his commanding officer- the Lord Viscount Iveagh (Arthur Magennis). Magennis is a distant relative of the Curtain/Macartan family, and he would likely have had long standing tribal ties to him. Phellim appears to be imprisoned with the remainder of his military garrison until the conclusion of the Confederate Wars in 1654, after which he was sold as a bondsman in Barbados for sedition against the Commonwealth. The likelihood of his survival in Barbados, like that of his peers, was extremely low, as the Irish prisoners of war often died before the completion of their sentence. There in Barbados he labored as a sugar slave on a plantation for around two years. By some unseen providence the Church Warden at St. John's, an Italian merchant named 'Fardinando Paleolagus', bought the title to Phellim's bondsmanship and released him from servitude. Paleolagus' reason for doing so is unknown, as these titles were often expensive, and there was no financial advantage to assuming and dissolving such a deed. However, given Paleolagus' own royalist and Catholic sympathies, his reasons may have been political, moral, if not altogether personal.

Phellim becomes a Freeman in 1656 or 1657. His whereabouts directly follow his release are unknown. He is not noted as dying on Barbados, and the passenger manifests for Barbados do not survive until later in the century. Just the same, he is not listed as being present in the religious census in Ireland in 1659, and it is unlikely that he returned to and Ireland still under the Cromwellian government. Curiously, he does not appear to be in the country until his restoration under King Charles II, where he is given a bill of unattaintment, restoring his former estates and holdings. He could have been seeking political asylum in Spain or France or assumed the role of a mercenary or brigand in the Caribbean or sojourned to the English charter colonies in North America. The spelling of his name makes it difficult, if not impossible, to identify his whereabouts, as Curtane/Curtain is rendered at least a dozen different ways in various surviving documents. His life after his military service is otherwise unknown.

He must have died before the Dutch Invasion in 1689, as he is not noted as being involved in any subsequent battle or political conflict. However, he must have lived long enough to have at least two sons, both of whom would build upon his political mantle. When and where they were born remains unclear, as Phellim's wife is not mentioned. He does not appear to be married at the time of his deportation in 1654, and there is no record of marriage taking place in Barbados. The nativity of his children and the identity of his wife are likely tied to where he resided during this otherwise unknown period. His son William is associated with the town of 'Doon' in County Limerick, which provides some potential insight, as this might suggest that his wife was an

English Catholic transplant to the region, or perhaps a member of the O'Grady gentry family who held an estate in Doon. This would further explain why the English transliteration of names appear to survive in subsequent generations, in stark contrast to the Gaelic names used in all previous generations.

Phellim's children that are known from the historical record are:

i. **Cornelius Curtain**, (*See Generation 31b below*)
ii. **William Curtain**, also known as Liam MacCurtain na-Duna (*See Generation 31c below*)
iii. **(Unnamed daughter)**, mother of Francis Kissane of Dromboy, Co. Cork, south of the townland of Mallow. She is said to have been the mother of at least a dozen children. However, their names are forgotten.
iv. **Margret Curtain(e)**, who married John Mahoney in 1677 near Carrignavar in Co. Cork.
v. **Daniel Curtain(e)**, who married Catherine Copps in 1680 in Cork City. His name is also rendered as "Daniell".

30c) Cornelius Curtain,

(Conchobhar MacCurtain)

son of GiollaPadraig son of Eogan son of Eachmilidh son of Phelim son of Turlogh son of Aedh son of Eachmilidh son of Giolla Colm son of Giolla Droigin son of Giolla Domnall son of Giolla Padraig son of Searran son of Tomas Oge son of Tomas Mor son of Sean son of Donnchad of son of Giolla Colm son of Cinnait son of Eochaid son of Domnall son of Giolla Colm son of Ciannait son of Raghnall son of Searran son of Eochaidh son of Concruach MacArtán, son of Crum na-Cruach MacArtán, son of Cuonincon MacArtán, son of Artán

This man, Fr. Cornelius Curtain, appears to have more information regarding his life than any previous member of the genealogy. The exact nature of his claim to fame is not particularly clear, beyond that he was a social contact for much of the native Gaelic literati. According to *Dánta Sheáin* his Gaelic name was 'Connor MacCurtain', and his literary achieves survived well into the 19th century in Irish, Latin and English. He is said to have translated the Latin catechism into Irish with the aid of many other priests. Among his students was the famous poet, Sean na-Raithineach. We are told that he was ordained into the Catholic clergy in 1684 by Pierce Creagh, Catholic Bishop of Cork, in Cork City Proper. He is noted as residing in a home in Coole in the North Liberties of Cork from 1691 to his death. Before his death he wrote the following elegy regarding his own life: "Beaneath this soil I sleep/the savant of Cairteanaigh/I who pursued wisdom and the arts/And excelled among the schools. Fare thee well, unclean earth/All the glory of the world is nothingness save the love of God."

> **Born:** 1658, Mallow, Co. Cork, Kingdom of Ireland
> **Died:** 1737, Coole, Co. Cork, Kingdom of Ireland
> Interred at: Teampoll Loircte
> **Occupation:** Parish Priest of Glanmire 1684-?, Parish Priest of Rathcony 1704(?)

> Sic perit Eous post plurima saecula Phoenix,
>   Sic se lamentans dulcis obivit Olor.
> Sic Aquila emoritur post mille per astra volatus,
>   Sic rosa marcescit, sic Philomela perit.
> Ergo jaces gelida, Demetri candide, in urna
>   Ah dilecte mihi caelicolisque senex !
> Te vivum colui, te cassum luce sequentur
>   Constanti studio vota, precesque, mea.

Elegy of Fr. Curtain, translated: You died, [and] after many centuries awoke as the Phoenix, sweet to meet the swan's cries. You face death after the flight of a thousand stars; [for] just as the rose fades, the nightingale also must die. Now, [you] lie motionless, in an urn, the heir of Demetrius. Oh, my dear, that ancient breath of life! You live [again] somewhere, residing in the light, in my constant prayers and wishes."

The infamous 'Flight of the Wild Geese from Limerick Harbor in 1692. Cornelius Curtain (Capt.) would have been involved in this exile.

31b) Cornelius Curtain,

son of Phelim son of GiollaPadraig son of Eogan son of Eachmilidh son of Phelim son of Turlogh son of Aedh son of Eachmilidh son of Giolla Colm son of Giolla Droigin son of Giolla Domnall son of Giolla Padraig son of Searran son of Tomas Oge son of Tomas Mor son of Sean son of Donnchad of son of Giolla Colm son of Cinnait son of Eochaid son of Domnall son of Giolla Colm son of Ciannait son of Raghnall son of Searran son of Eochaidh son of Concruach MacArtán, son of Crum na-Cruach MacArtán, son of Cuonincon MacArtán, son of Artán

His birth name would likely be *Conchobar MacCurtain* in its original Gaelic form. However, any services to the Peerage of the Kingdom of Ireland requires an English transliteration of the birth name. His father, '*Phellim Curtane*', was already tied to the tumult of the 17th century. It was during his childhood that the MacCurtain was restored of his family lands in 1662 by King Charles II following the large confiscation by the Cromwellian administration. No ecclesiastical records survive of his life, as most Catholic church had been destroyed a generation prior during the Cromwellian Invasion. He appears to have been educated, although to what degree is not clear. He spoke French with some regularity, so it might be assumed that his formal education was either in France proper or at the hands of a French cleric. The English records do list in on two different occasions as a "gentleman", that meaning a landowner. He is listed as being a member of the Irish Army of King James II in 1689, and was personally present at the siege of Limerick, as well as the king's defeat at the Battle of the Boyne. His rank is listed as "Captain", in the service of Major General Alexandre de Rainier de Droue, Marquis de

Boisseleau's Infantry division in 1690. His home township is listed twice, once as "Mellyforttown", and later as "Mallyfanstowne", both times this township is said to be in northern County Cork. The former rendering of the name appears to be an archaic phrasing of the township now known as Milford in County Cork, although it is possible that this could also be the city of Mallow. No historic record notes this township, so it is unclear. In a French record of his great-grandson, he is called Cornelius Curtain of Muckrooa, Co. Cork. However, this locale is not identifiable at all. His ancestry is never specified, although one French source notes a grandfather/great-grandfather, Tomas, who was killed during the Williamite War in Ireland, likely around 1690. He is listed as among those pardoned by William III and Mary II in 1690 and appeared to temporarily hold onto his landholdings. The English record does not specify if this pardon was requested, or just granted to the natives as means of reconciliation following the Williamite War. Whatever the case may be, the peace is short lived, as he had left Ireland with the Jacobite Army of 19,000 Irishmen under the Earl of Lucan in 1691. He appears to have returned in Ireland in 1696 during the Jacobite attempt to depose the Williamite government. For this he was placed under royal attaint in 1696 (the state confiscation of his property and civil liberties). Subsequent to this, he appears to skip the country, rendering his services as an officer to the French Crown under Louis XIV. William III by royal act attainted him, along with his colleagues, a second time in 1697 for his allegiance to the Jacobite cause and to the French state. He appears to have remained in France after 1697 at Charleroi (now part of Belgium). However, beyond his military service, very little is known of his life in France. He was a participant in the war of Spanish Succession in 1700 and appears to have survived the conflict. He is noted as having been widowed prior to his second marriage in 1699 to an unnamed French woman. The name of his second wife is unknown, and no French church records have been found to document this nuptial. His first wife appears in connection with his peer, Philip Cogan, a Captain of Infantrymen under the same Jacobite company. She is called "Catherine", and hails from the Anglo-Irish family that sat in on the "Native parliament" of 1689. The details of her life are unknown otherwise. He appears to be the brother or son of a certain John Curtain who is forced to register with the English magistrate in Co. Cork in 1692. Cornelius' relationship to the Catholic Priest, Rev. Cornelius Curtain (*or Connor MacCurtain*), who hails from Coole in northern Cork is also a curiosity. He is clearly a separate individual, as the clerical Cornelius was ordained in 1684, and is found in registries as being active in the diocese as a clerical regular in 1704. If any familial relationship exists, it is unknown at this current moment in time. The last reference to his life comes from the Criminal Courts in Dublin, namely the Court of the Exchequer, where it is noted that he is placed on trial alongside an unknown man surnamed Dillon and the Lord Mayor of Cork City. The former individual might be connected to Cornelius' charges. The court record states that he was charged with "sheltering a popish dignitary", which then a state offence at the time. It is unclear what this means, beyond that he was assisting Catholic clergy move about Ireland without formal state registration in Dublin. He was detained at Dublin Castle for about two years before being executed. According to the English record, his last words are said to be a prayer to God.

Born: abt. 1660/1665, around what is now Mallow, Co. Cork.

Died: Dec. 1, 1724, Dublin Castle, Dublin, Kingdom of Ireland, killed by "hanging of the neck until dead"

Occupation: Royal Army of the Kingdom of Ireland 1689-1696, 1st Battalion of King James' Royal Irish Footguards 1696-1698, Irish Brigade of the Kingdom of France 1698-?, French Civil Servant 1700 (?) or so

Married: 1st Wife- CATHERINE O'DONOVAN, daughter of DONAL O'DONOVAN and ELIZABETH TONSON, likely in the old church of the Holy Cross in Rath Luirc. 2nd Wife- Joanne Quinn, a Franco-Irish Woman, or perhaps someone tied to the MacCarthy family.

CAPTAIN CORNELIUS CURTAIN.

HE was attainted in 1696, by the description of Cornelius 'Curtan' of Mellyforttown, County Cork, Gent., and the name is still known in that county.

Children of CORNELIUS CURTAIN and CATHERINE O'DONOVAN:

i)   **Cornelius Curtain**, (*See Generation 33a below*) had issue
ii)   **Mary Curtain**,
iii)   **John Curtain**, He stands alone as having a baptismal record. He was christened Jean François Jacques Macartan on May 31, 1692 at Rennes, Duchy of Brittany, Kingdom of France. He is stated as residing in France on April 16, 1714 for the wedding of a friend/cousin, Capt. Charles MacCarthy

and Jeanne MacCarthy. In this billing he is noted as 'Jean Curtain'. He is again referenced in a wedding party of Jacobites in France on January 7, 1717, where his occupation is noted as Captain in the Irish Army. His fate thereafter is unknown. If he has descendants, they are likely to be in northern France. It appears that the family estates, whatever of them remained after 1689, were passed to his brothers: Simon, William and Gabriel, all of who converted to the Church of Ireland.

iv) **Simon Curtain**, after 1690, before 1699, married Catherine Mansfield in 1718 in Co. Cork. Their whereabouts thereafter are unknown. Her baptismal record appears to survive, as she was christened at Saint Michael's Catholic church on March 19, 1681 in the city of Dublin. Simon is mentioned as being reimbursed for repairing the city clock, but he does not appear to have any other civil distinction in his lifetime. A son named John is mentioned on the Cork City Council in 1750. Simon is also referenced as being alive well until 1778. This seems improbable, as he would be almost 90 years old. Therefore, we might assume that he had another son of this same name. However, there do not appear to be any references to him beyond passing probate records. It is likely that he had converted to the Church of Ireland to assume his civic post and to hold the title of "freeman". The name Simon is rarely used amongst the Irish, its employment here is likely referential to his date of birth, which would be October 28th, the feast of St. Simon the Canaanite.

v) **Hanora Curtain**, born after 1690 but before 1699. She is said to have been born at Balimbalig, north of Cork City. Hanora, also called Eleanor, married James MacMahon, later known as 'Diego'. He became a Wildgoose in the service of the Spanish crown. They had two children Patrick MacMahon and Terence MacMahon. Their descendants are extremely prolific and found across various Latin America nations. She and her husband died in 1748 in Shandon, Co. Cork, Kingdom of Ireland.

vi) **Anne Curtain**, born after 1690, before 1699

vii) **Bartholomew Curtain**, (*See Generation 33b below*) possibly born in the Kingdom of France.

viii) **Catherine Curtain**, her name is too common to determine any features of her life.

ix) **William Curtain**, born around 1700. Married July 20, 1725, Church of Saint John, Limerick City, Co. Limerick, Kingdom of Ireland, to Mary Strange. He is misbilled as 'William Curtny' in the official ecclesiastical record. William appears to be akin to several of his siblings, as this is an Anglican church, and Mary Strange appears to be an English colonist in the region. It is unknown if they have any children.

x) **Gabriel Curtain,** who is mentioned as splitting an inheritance with his eldest brother Cornelius in 1724 from a distant relative. His later whereabouts are unspecified. He might be the same as the 'Anton Gabrielo Curtina' who appears in Gerona, Spain at this time, although this is unlikely. A Gabriel Curtin is found residing in Dunbullig, outside of Carrignavar in 1755 in probate records. However, no peripheral family members are noted. Given that Gabriel is permitted to inherit property and is listed as being a property holder himself, he too is likely a convert to the Church of Ireland during this time. It is unclear whether he was married or had children, no records appear to survive, and his name 'Gabriel' is unusual for this period. Given its rarity in Irish use, it is likely that he was born on the commemoration of the feast of St. Gabriel, March 18th.

Irish Bard, 17th century

31c)   William Curtain,

son of Phelim son of GiollaPadraig son of Eogan son of Eachmilidh son of Phelim son of Turlogh son of Aedh son of Eachmilidh son of Giolla Colm son of Giolla Droigin son of Giolla Domnall son of Giolla Padraig son of Searran son of Tomas Oge son of Tomas Mor son of Sean son of Donnchad of son of Giolla Colm son of Cinnait son of Eochaid son of Domnall son of Giolla Colm son of Ciannait son of Raghnall son of Searran son of Eochaidh son of Concruach MacArtán, son of Crum na-Cruach MacArtán, son of Cuonincon MacArtán, son of Artán

He is perhaps best known as Liam MacCurtain na-Duna, or at times Uilliam MacCarteinn. His place of nativity is uncertain, some source again note that he was born in Ulster, but this might be taken from a similar source as Fr. Cornelius Curtain's genealogy. We know of his military service during the Williamite war, and that he participated in a battle at Beal Atha Salainn on April 29th 1691. He is mentioned in the will of his uncle, the priest, although he is apparently deceased, and his inheritance went to his widow. On the death of Diarmaid MacCarthy in 1705 he assumed control of the Gaelic school at

Carrignavar. Moreover, William was an extensive writer and translator, and allegedly had a substantial education. He had participated in the compilation of the poems of Ossian with James macPherson in the early 18th century. Some of his poems appear to have survived to this current day and have been recently translated into Gaelic. The subject of his poems addresses the de-invested Irish gentry and the expulsion of various Catholic bishops and clergymen. He appears to have endorsed the same cause of his brother, but sought more legal challenges to address the shifting political and social powers in the region. He notes the loss of familial prestige in the opening lines of one of his poems, saying "through riches and wealth, I have none, I squandered and lost them too soon, I cherish the friendship of one, Who is constant, kind-hearted and true."

> **Born:** 1668, Kingdom of Ireland, (at times his birth is noted as 1658, however this appears to be in error)
> **Died:** November 1724, Carrignavar, Co. Cork, Kingdom of Ireland
> **Occupation:** Chief of the Bardic School in Carrignavar 1705-1724, Cavalrymen in the Army of King James II (non-officer) 1688-1691, Unspecified Courtier to the Earl of Desmond 1691-1705
> **Married:** Catherin Aherin

Children of WILLIAM CURTAIN and CATHERIN AHERIN:

i)   **Donall Curtain**, nothing is known regarding the life of Donall, but his son John/Sean took up the mantle of the bardic tradition in the late 18th century. However, he did not gain the notoriety of his grandfather. The many Curtins of Carrignavar appear to primarily descend through this son of William. Unfortunately, records are limited in the 18th century and the precise nature of this descent remains unclear.

ii)   **Cornelius Curtain**, *(See Article VI, Generation 32)*

iii)   **Joseph Curtain**, also known as Ioreph MacCurtain, he later became the parish priest of Carrignavar. He is described as living as "saintly life" of "irreproachable virtue". A legend appears regarding his life that he was attacked by an evil spirit while tending to the sick near Lyre in the middle of the night. In the process of fighting off this unclean spirit he neck became twisted and deformed. Although the record is unclear whether this was truly an encounter with the demonic or a stroke of paralysis. He died in 1752 and was buried in the God's acre in Dunbulloge. None of his writings appear to have survived to the present day. His headstone appears to have stood until the early 20th century, which stated "Here lyeth the body of the Rev. Joseph Curtain, Parish Priest of Dunbolg who departed this life the 20th of Jan. 1752 in ye 56th year of his age". Sean na-Raithineach wrote the following elegy for his passing: "Beneath this sod, alas, now lies/this saintly poet and scholar wise,/brave yet gentle, kind and good, Joseph mac Cairteain of noble blood."

Article II:
"Kind Hearts and Coronets"
The Senior Line of French Curtins
1685-1870

32a)   Cornelius (Mac)Curtain,

*son of Cornelius, son of Phelim son of GiollaPadraig son of Eogan son of
Eachmilidh son of Phelim son of Turlogh son of Aedh son of Eachmilidh son of
Giolla Colm son of Giolla Droigin son of Giolla Domnall son of Giolla Padraig son
of Searran son of Tomas Oge son of Tomas Mor son of Sean son of Donnchad of
son of Giolla Colm son of Cinnait son of Eochaid son of Domnall son of Giolla
Colm son of Ciannait son of Raghnall son of Searran son of Eochaidh son of
Concruach MacArtán, son of Crum na-Cruach MacArtán, son of Cuonincon
MacArtán, son of Artán*

This younger Cornelius Curtain is said to have married Joanna Coppinger in
1722 in Co. Cork, Ireland. His home parish is listed as 'Ballymacgooly',
which is now part of Mallow township in Northern Cork. She is said to hail
from Christ Church parish which is located within the confines of Cork City

proper. How they met or under what terms they were married is lost to time. The civil records indicate that he employed the post-nomen "Junior" to his name, which would suggest that his father was still living at the time of this marriage. However, little is known of his life beyond these short details. If he maintained any political sympathies, he did an excellent job at not having them be made public. His eldest child was born in Cork in 1724, but his whereabouts after this period are unclear. In this same year, we find the last will and testament of a distant relative of Cornelius who grants him his estate in full. Given the nature of this estate, it appears that Cornelius lived in moderate wealth for much of his life. He appears to have abandoned the claims to his family estate in Mallow or Milford, and resettled near his wife's family in Cork City. Beyond his ties to his brother, Gabriel Curtain, he does not appear to hold any personal ties to his younger siblings.

Born: abt. 1685 in Co. Cork, Ireland
Died: after 1724, likely in the Kingdom of France
Married: Joanna Coppinger, Nov. 10, 1722, probably at Christ Church, Cork City, Co. Cork, Ireland

Children of CORNELIUS (MAC)CURTAIN AND JOANNA COPPINGER:

i.   **Cornelius (Mac)Curtain**, born 1724 in Co. Cork, Ireland. (*See Generation 34a below*)

ii.   **Alice Curtain**, married Nicholas Halfpenny (born 1716), an English Merchant and Adventurer, in 1741. He may be the same man who would latter work as architect on the barrack at Castleisland, Co. Kerry in 1757. However, even English sources do not appear to be certain.

iii.   **Daniel Curtain,** born 1733 in Co. Cork, Ireland. He married Margaret Nagle and had at least one son: **William Curtain** in 1757, a merchant in Cork City. This occupation may have been a matter of exposure from his uncle, Nicholas Halfpenny. William Curtain resides in Cork City for the entirety of his short life, dying in 1785 at the age of 28. Before he died he married a local woman, Margaret Deasy, and had one posthumous child, **Margaret Honoria Curtain** in 1786. This Margaret appears to have had a destiny that ties to Curtain Clan to the Anglo-Norman blood of the sovereign House of Windsor.

The life of Margaret Honoris Curtain stands alone from that of all other Curtins noted in this text. She starts life with the indefinitely disadvantage of being born to a mother and deceased father. There is no civil record or church baptism regarding her birth, only that it is noted that she was born in 1786 in Cork City, Kingdom of Ireland. Her life is otherwise ordinary, save only her choice of spouse, who in this case was the Anglo-Irish Officer, Edward Roche (1771-1855). The civil registry states they married in July 1805, within the Catholic Church, in the Diocese of Cork & Ross. Margaret appears to have attained some role of socialite within the City of Cork before her marriage, and is often associated with a relative of unclear relation, the Hon. Edmund Burke. Together the couple has two children, Frances Maria Roche, who marries James Kelly in 1834, and Edmund Burke, who is granted the title of 1st Lord of Fermoy in 1865. Perhaps his political rise would be token enough of his fortune, but this same Edmund Burke is ancestor of great-great grandfather to Diana Spencer, Princess of Wales. And thus, the current Duke of Cambridge, and his brother the Duke of Sussex, are in direct descent from this Captain Cornelius Curtain, the supposed ancestor of the Curtin Clan of County Cork.

33a) Cornelius MacCurtain,

son of Cornelius, son of Cornelius, son of Phelim son of GiollaPadraig son of Eogan son of Eachmilidh son of Phelim son of Turlogh son of Aedh son of Eachmilidh son of Giolla Colm son of Giolla Droigin son of Giolla Domnall son of Giolla Padraig son of Searran son of Tomas Oge son of Tomas Mor son of Sean son of Donnchad of son of Giolla Colm son of Cinnait son of Eochaid son of Domnall son of Giolla Colm son of Ciannait son of Raghnall son of Searran son of Eochaidh son of Concruach MacArtán, son of Crum na-Cruach MacArtán, son of Cuonincon MacArtán, son of Artán

He is said to have emigrated to Nantes, France sometime after his birth, although the reason for this passage are explained in no record. Religious and political persecution might be presumed, but not explicit. He was recruited into the infamous 'Wild-Geese', in the 2nd Clare Infantryman, which would have promised political and financial opportunity for the family. Or perhaps, alternatively, this was untaken by this Cornelius as he reached the age of maturity and was able to consent to military service. In either case, he was able to attain success, being knighted by King Louis XV, and granted the title 'Sieur de Kainlis' (Knight of Kainlis). This is not entrance to the French national peerage, but it is granted to individuals for excellent service to the French Crown. His descendants appear to continue the tradition of involvement in French State politics for the next century.

Born: 1724, Co. Cork, Ireland
Died: Unknown, likely in Nantes, France
Occupation: Civil Servant (?), Solider in the Irish Brigade of the French Army (?)
Married: 1st wife, Victoire Le Tellier de Grandval; 2nd wife, Marie Sophie Peloteau

Children of CORNELIUS MACCURTAIN and VICTOIRE LE TELLIER DE GRANDVAL:
i.   **Florimond Benjamin MacCurtain de Kainlis**, born 1764, France. (*See Generation 35a below*)

Children of CORNELIUS MACCURTAIN and MARIE SOPHIE PELOTEAU:
ii.   **Francois Marie MacCurtain**, born 1775. Beyond the mention of her birth, nothing else is known about her or her later life.

Signature of Florimond-Benjamin MacCurtain, circa 1830. No portrait appears to survive of him in the public record.

34a) Florimond Benjamin MacCurtain,

son of Cornelius, son of Cornelius, son of Cornelius, son of Phelim son of GiollaPadraig son of Eogan son of Eachmilidh son of Phelim son of Turlogh son of Aedh son of Eachmilidh son of Giolla Colm son of Giolla Droigin son of Giolla Domnall son of Giolla Padraig son of Searran son of Tomas Oge son of Tomas Mor son of Sean son of Donnchad of son of Giolla Colm son of Cinnait son of Eochaid son of Domnall son of Giolla Colm son of Ciannait son of Raghnall son of Searran son of Eochaidh son of Concruach MacArtán, son of Crum na-Cruach MacArtán, son of Cuonincon MacArtán, son of Artán

He is perhaps the most successful of all of the French Curtins. He entered military services in the French Royal Army in 1781 at seventeen years of age. He was quickly granted the rank of 'Commissioner of War' within the Army, and elected deputy of the Loire-Inferior to the Council of Five Hundred. During the revolution he was sentenced to deportation because of his father's status as a knight and landowner but was able to escape from this and join the Chouans. He campaigned for the royalists in Upper Britany and Lower Anjou for some time. During the French Consulate, he was relieved of his duties and remained out of public affairs during the age and chaos of Napoleon. Following the restoration of the French monarchy he was permitted to rejoin the legitimist Army of Louis XVIII in 1814, and appointed military superintendent on October 4, 1820, an office which he held until his retirement on June 7, 1834. He was granted the Barony of Kainlis for his service to the French Crown, as well as the distinction of an 'Officer of the Legion of Honor'.

> **Born:** July 29, 1764, Savennieres, Maine-et-Loire, Kingdom of France
> **Died:** 1857, Kingdom of France
> **Occupation:** French Military Officer, 1781-1797, 1814-1834, Created Baron de Kainlis on May 28, 1825 by King Charles X of France.

Married: Marie Anne Aubin de l'Estang; born: 1770, Unknown, died: April 19, 1816, Indre-et-Loire, Centre, Kingdom of France

Children of FLORIMOND MACCURTAIN and MARIE ANNE AUBIN DE L'ESTANG:

i.   **Cornelie Victorie MacCurtain de Kainlis**, born 1794, died 1817. She was briefly married to Francois Michel Le Febre de Montifray before her premature death. She does not appear to have any issue, and his death appears to rather sudden.

ii.   **Marie Sidonie MacCurtain de Kainlis**, born 1805, died Jan. 10, 1870. She was twice married to: Auguste Raoul Cassin on October 7, 1823 until his death on Jan. 11, 1836, and then to Amedee Cassin in 1844. She is buried with her second husband at the Church of Dangé-Saint-Romain in Vienne, France, on the border with the Swiss Confederation. By Raoul de Cassin she has three sons: Alfred de Cassin (?-1853), Gustave de Cassin (1827-1895), and Oscar de Cassin (1833-1914). She appears to be heavily involved in philanthropic movements and in supporting the early French Archeological Society in its various expeditions to Egypt and the Levant. Although it is not clear to what extent, she does appear to be known and in the social circles of Emperor Napoleon III.

Following the death of Marie Sidonie this line becomes extinct. While she does have descendants, they are of the House of deCassin. Their place within the old French Peerage appears to be preserved until the time of the First World War, when their titular possession of 'Baron deKainlis' was abandoned. However, Florimond MacCurtain is still honored as a hero of the French State and is not an unknown name within 19th century French history.

Article III:
"The Wild Rover"
Curtins amongst the Choctaw Indians
1763-Present

32c) Cornelius McCurtain,

Son of William, son of Phelim son of GiollaPadraig son of Eogan son of Eachmilidh son of Phelim son of Turlogh son of Aedh son of Eachmilidh son of Giolla Colm son of Giolla Droigin son of Giolla Domnall son of Giolla Padraig son of Searran son of Tomas Oge son of Tomas Mor son of Sean son of Donnchad of son of Giolla Colm son of Cinnait son of Eochaid son of Domnall son of Giolla Colm son of Ciannait son of Raghnall son of Searran son of Eochaidh son of Concruach MacArtán, son of Crum na-Cruach MacArtán, son of Cuonincon MacArtán, son of Artán

There appears to be some confusion regarding the life of Cornelius. It appears that he is two separate men- Cornelius Sr and Cornelius Jr. However, separating the two of them is exceedingly difficult given the sparse reference to their lives. We know that he was residing in Co. Cork Ireland well into his twenties, as his children are noted as being born in Ireland itself. He must have volunteered for the Wildgeese sometime after 1750. His reasons for doing so are obscured by history. He does not appear in the 1766 Religious Census of Co. Cork. It appears that he remained in service to the Spanish crown sometime before 1763, as he obtained a homestead through their charter. In 1763 the treaty of Paris was signed, and Florida became a British territory, and thus Cornelius would have been unable to obtain a veteran's homestead in the Spanish colonial empire. It is assumed that he met his wife in Ireland, but her surname is obscured, and it is unclear how it was originally transcribed. We might assume that his life was particularly Spartan given the locale that he elected to settle in. He must have had strong social ties to the local Indian tribes of the region and engaged them in mutually beneficial transactions. This would not have been unusually, as the Spanish governor of West Florida, Arturo O'Neill was also an Irishman in Spanish military service. He may have participated in the Battle of Pensacola in 1781, where there was a heavy presence of the Irish Regiment.

> **Born:** 1722, Co. Cork, Kingdom of Ireland
> **Died:** about 1787. Colony of West Florida, Kingdom of Spain
> **Married:** Hanora Hecha (or Heche, or Hechadre) in 1745 or 1746. She was born 1728, Co. Cork, Kingdom of Ireland; died: 1818, Mississippi, United States of America. Alternatively, she is stated to have died in Ireland, although this appears unlikely. Familiarly, she was referred to as "Annie".
> **Occupation:** Solider in the Irish Brigade of the Spanish Army 'Regimento Hibernia'

Children of CORNELIUS MCCURTAIN and HANORA HECHA:
i)   **Cornelius McCurtain**, born Mar. 23, 1747. *(See Section VIII below)*
ii)   **Daniel McCurtain**, born July 1748 *(See Section VIII below)*
iii)   **Francis McCurtain**, born 1750, died in 1790. It is unclear whether he had issue or not. There are no surviving records that specify this.
iv)   **Thomas McCurtain,** mistaken in some genealogies as the father of Daniel McCurtain. The particulars of his own lifetime are obscured. He also might be a son of the younger Cornelius.

Choctaw Indian in Spanish Florida, circa 1810

33c)   Daniel McCurtain,

Son of Cornelius, son of William, son of Phelim son of GiollaPadraig son of Eogan son of Eachmilidh son of Phelim son of Turlogh son of Aedh son of Eachmilidh son of Giolla Colm son of Giolla Droigin son of Giolla Domnall son of Giolla Padraig son of Searran son of Tomas Oge son of Tomas Mor son of Sean son of Donnchad of son of Giolla Colm son of Cinnait son of Eochaid son of Domnall son of Giolla Colm son of Ciannait son of Raghnall son of Searran son of Eochaidh son of Concruach MacArtán, son of Crum na-Cruach MacArtán, son of Cuonincon MacArtán, son of Artán

Daniel's animosity to the British Empire must have been palpable. When the American Revolution broke-out he traveled north to fight at the Battle of Lexington in 1775. He is listed as being discharged from the Continental Army on May 29, 1776. He thereafter joined militia men and assisted with the capture of Saratoga, New York on April 17, 1777. He remained with Daniel Morgan's riffle battalion until the end of the war. He allegedly kept a journal of his experiences, called 'Journal of the Siege of Boston'. Daniel's life appears to be obscured following the revolution. He appears to be invested in most of his time in Maryland, never returning to the Florida frontier. For that reason, it is not clear what relationship he had with his son or wife, as they appear to have remained behind in Florida. Moreover, Daniel is noted as serving in a German Battalion in the Continental Army, for reasons that are unclear. This might be a catch-all for individuals who did not hold English ancestry. It is suggested that he did not know that he had a son, and therefore did not see any need to return.

        Born: July 1748, Co. Cork, Kingdom of Ireland
        Died: 1830, Kent County, State of Maryland, United States of America
        U.S. Revolutionary War Roll: Enlisted Oct. 6, 1776, Continental Troops, German Battalion, Sergeant
        U.S. Revolutionary War Roll: March 1, 1777, Continental Troops, German Battalion, Quarter Master Sergeant
        U.S. Census 1790: Kent County, Maryland
        U.S. Census 1800: Kent County, Maryland
        Married: *1st marriage*, Celia Jane (NO LAST NAME); born about 1760, died 1814. The exact whereabouts of their marriage is unclear. They wed in 1777 in what was then land claimed by the state of Georgia (but now constitutes Mississippi). She was a full-blood member of the Choctaw Indian nation.
        2nd marriage, Ann Becha (born Hannah Kennedy, or Hannag Scelia?). She was born 1758. She was another full-blood member of the Choctaw Indian nation, born under French sovereignty in the region around 1750. They had no offspring.
        Occupation: Homesteader, American Soldier in the Continental Army 1776-1783

        Children of DANIEL MCCURTAIN and CELIA JANE:
        i)   **Daniel McCurtain**, born July 6, 1777 (see Generation 34b).

LaMobile City Plan (now Mobile, Alabama) circa 1750

33d)   Cornelius McCurtain,

Son of Cornelius, son of William, son of Phelim son of GiollaPadraig son of Eogan son of Eachmilidh son of Phelim son of Turlogh son of Aedh son of Eachmilidh son of Giolla Colm son of Giolla Droigin son of Giolla Domnall son of Giolla Padraig son of Searran son of Tomas Oge son of Tomas Mor son of Sean son of Donnchad of son of Giolla Colm son of Cinnait son of Eochaid son of Domnall son of Giolla Colm son of Ciannait son of Raghnall son of Searran son of Eochaidh son of Concruach MacArtán, son of Crum na-Cruach MacArtán, son of Cuonincon MacArtán, son of Artán

Cornelius appears to have immersed himself in the world of the French colonists along the Gulf of Mexico. Both of his wives are taken from these ranks. He must have been a multilingual man as his first wife, Marguerite LeFleau, only spoke French. He must have known both, English, Spanish, and French, and perhaps Gaelic, as well as various native American tongues to successfully conduct trade in the region. His will survives which attests to the extent of his formal education and penmanship. In his will he professes his Catholic faith and his native heritage to the Irish nation.

He does not appear to be interested in the developed United States, which was becoming a growing political reality to the north of his home. In his lifetime his national loyalty change because of the shifting geography. In 1763, LaMobile was ceded to the United Kingdom, in 1783 in was ceded to Spain, and at the end of his life, in 1813, it was annexed to the United States. His attachment to Ireland and being of Irish ancestry appears to be non-existent, as the name of his children appear to reflect a French and American influence.
    Born: Mar. 23, 1747, Co. Cork, Kingdom of Ireland

Died: 1814, Mobile, Territory of West Florida, Kingdom of Spain (now the State of Alabama); interred: Immaculate Cathedral Graveyard, Mobile, Territory of West Florida

Religious census of 1796-1801: Cornelio McCurtain, Precept list for the Diocese of Pensacola

Occupation: Merchant, Chief of the Moshulatubbee region, Choctaw Nation (?)

Additional Information: He appears to have obtained a homestead of his own from Major Robert Farmer, upon his death in 1778, near what is now Stockton, Alabama. He was also the Godfather of Adam Cornelius Hollinger. The claim that he was a Choctaw Chief seems unlikely, as he neither has this in his blood, nor does he intermarry with the local Choctaw tribes.

Married: *1st Wife*- Margarite LeFleau, Nov. 24, 1778, Immaculate Conception Catholic Church, LaMobile, Territory of West Florida, Kingdom of France. The child of Jean Baptiste LeFleau and Marie Jeanne Girard of LaMobile. She was born July 4, 1760 in LaMobile, Kingdom of France. Died August 1787, Dauphne Saint-Mobile, Territory of West Florida, Kingdom of Spain.

2nd Wife- Marie Eufrosina Bousages, January 20, 1806, Mobile, Territory of West Florida, Kingdom of Spain. The child of Joseph Bosarge and Catherine Louise Baudreau. She was born in 1777 in Mobile, Territory of West Florida, United Kingdom. Died July 11, 1845, Mobile, Alabama, United States. Buried at Magnolia Cemetery, Mobile, Alabama. They must have divorced shortly thereafter, as she went on to marry a man named Diego McVoy in 1808. They had no children together.

Children of CORNELIUS MCCURTAIN and MARGARITE LEFLEAU:
i)   **Jackson McCurtain,** born 1782
ii)   **Edmond MacCurtain,** born 1784
iii)   **Green McCurtain,** born 1786
iv)   **Louis McCurtain,** born August 1787. His mother died ten days later from complications of childbirth.

34b)   Daniel McCurtain,

Son of Daniel, son of Cornelius, son of William, son of Phelim son of GiollaPadraig son of Eogan son of Eachmilidh son of Phelim son of Turlogh son of Aedh son of Eachmilidh son of Giolla Colm son of Giolla Droigin son of Giolla Domnall son of Giolla Padraig son of Searran son of Tomas Oge son of Tomas Mor son of Sean son of Donnchad of son of Giolla Colm son of Cinnait son of Eochaid son of Domnall son of Giolla Colm son of Ciannait son of Raghnall son of Searran son of Eochaidh son of Concruach MacArtán, son of Crum na-Cruach MacArtán, son of Cuonincon MacArtán, son of Artán

He assumed the name "Pataley" and was deeply devoted to the Choctaw Nation, presumably through his stepmother. His father, also named Daniel McCurtain, appears to have largely abandoned the boy and let him be raised by his 2nd wife's relations. For this reason, he embraced the Choctaw nation and identified as a native son of the tribe. In 1831, he sold his land along the Natchen Trace, some 640 acres that he had been granted for fighting in the War of 1812. He appears to have taken an interest in the tribal affairs of the Choctaw nation, whom he descended from through his mother's family. He relocated his family to the Indian territory, Sugar Loaf County following this. He is noted as being present as an interpreter at the Treaty od Doaksville in 1837. He apparently was a shrewd businessman and sold his land for double its value by waiting for market prices to rise.

Born: July 6, 1777, Territory of West Florida, Kingdom of Spain
Died: Feb. 6, 1842, Sugarload (of Skullyville), Indian Territory, United States; Interred: Red Oak Cemetery, Red Oak, Latimer County, Indian Territory, United States
Occupation: U.S. Army 1812-1815, Captain
Married: Hannah Cole in 1800. She was born in Nov. 9, 1781, Territory of West Florida. Died June 8, 1843, Sugarloaf, Indian Territory, United States. Her father's identity is unclear, but her mother was Shamoka, a Shakchihoma Indian.
U.S. Census 1790: Residing in Kent Co., Maryland
Additional Information: They appear to have had an arranged marriage, although the ancestry of Hannah appears uncertain. She likely had Choctaw Indian blood as well.

Children of DANIEL MCCURTAIN and UNKNOWN WOMAN:
i)   **(Thomas) Elam McCurtain**, born 1795
ii)   **Daniel McCurtain**, born 1800. This Daniel must have been the eldest given Irish naming customs. However, nothing is recorded about his life and he may have died young.

Children of DANIEL MCCURTAIN and HANNAH COLE:
iii)   **Thomas McCurtain**, born 1801, who's fate is unknown to history.
iv)   **Cornelius McCurtain**, born 1803 (*See Generation 35b below*)
v)   **David Cornelius McCurtain**, born 1803
vi)   **Sophia McCurtain**, born 1810
vii)   **Luke McCurtain**, born 1812
viii)   **William McCurtain**, born 1814, (*See Generation 35c below*)
ix)   **Samuel Mitchell McCurtain**, born 1814
x)   **Allen McCurtain**, born 1818, who's fare is unknown to history
xi)   **Kemper McCurtain**, born 1820

35b) Cornelius McCurtain,

*Son of Daniel, son of Daniel, son of
Cornelius, son of William, son of
Phelim son of GiollaPadraig son of
Eogan son of Eachmilidh son of
Phelim son of Turlogh son of Aedh
son of Eachmilidh son of Giolla Colm
son of Giolla Droigin son of Giolla
Domnall son of Giolla Padraig son of
Searran son of Tomas Oge son of
Tomas Mor son of Sean son of
Donnchad of son of Giolla Colm son
of Cinnait son of Eochaid son of
Domnall son of Giolla Colm son of
Ciannait son of Raghnall son of
Searran son of Eochaidh son of
Concruach MacArtán, son of Crum
na-Cruach MacArtán, son of
Cuonincon MacArtán, son of Artán*

Cornelius experienced the removal of
Choctaws from modern Mississippi in
1833. He settled with his mother near Ft.
Coffee, where he was able to ply his trades farming and raising livestock. In
1849, he joined the board of trustees in the Moshulatubbe District and helped
with the chartering of schools in the area. That same year he was elected
Choctaw Chief of the First District, which he held until 1854. He was heavily
invested in tribal politics and often sought to preserve the autonomy of the
Choctaw nation. His children appear to have continued this legacy, many of
whom would go on to hold the title of 'chief' themselves.

> **Born:** March 5, 1803, Takuawa, Okla-Falaya District, Choctaw
> Nation East (Territory of Mississippi)
> **Died:** March 5, 1871, Choctaw nation West, Indian Territory, United
> States; Interred: Red Oak Cemetery, Red Oak, Latimer County,
> Indian Territory, United States
> **Occupation:** Chief of the Choctaw Nation
> **Married:** Mahayia Bevlin "amy" in 1826. She was born in PAril 30,
> 1806, Choctaw nation East. Died Oct. 23, 1872, Choctaw nation West
> Indian Territory, United States. Interred: Ludi Cemetery
> **Additional Information:** Mahayia's surname is also given as
> Nelson. "Belvin" might be an attempt to transliterate this.

Children of CORNELIUS MCCURTAIN and MAHAYIA BELVIN:
i)   **Jackson Frazier McCurtain**, born 1830. Died 1885.
        Married Marie Riley in 1851. He later became a chief of the
        Choctaw nation.
ii)   **Sina McCurtain**, born 1831, died 1835.

iii)   **Isabelle McCurtain**, born 1839, died 1873. She married George Riddle sometime after the American Civil War.

iv)   **Edmond A. McCurtain,** born 1842. Died 1890. He married Susan King. He later became a chief of the Choctaw nation.

v)   **David C. McCurtain,** born 1846

vi)   **Greenwood McCurtain,** born November 28, 1848

vii)   **Robert McCurtain,** born 1850

viii)   **Elsie McCurtain,** born 1851, died 1875. Married George Riddle in 1873, presumably directly following the death of her sister.

Grave of Mahayia McCurtain in Oklahoma

35c) William McCurtain,

Son of Daniel, son of Daniel, son of Cornelius, son of William, son of Phelim son of GiollaPadraig son of Eogan son of Eachmilidh son of Phelim son of Turlogh son of Aedh son of Eachmilidh son of Giolla Colm son of Giolla Droigin son of Giolla Domnall son of Giolla Padraig son of Searran son of Tomas Oge son of Tomas Mor son of Sean son of Donnchad of son of Giolla Colm son of Cinnait son of Eochaid son of Domnall son of Giolla Colm son of Ciannait son of Raghnall son of Searran son of Eochaidh son of Concruach MacArtán, son of Crum na-Cruach MacArtán, son of Cuonincon MacArtán, son of Artán

William served in the American Civil War under his nephew, Jackson Frazier McCurtain. He appears to be partially involved in the political on-goings of the Choctaw nation during his long lifetime.

Born: 1814, Takuawa, Okla-Falaya District, Choctaw Nation East (Territory of Mississippi)
Died: 1897, Choctaw nation West, Indian Territory, United States; Interred: Red Oak Cemetery, Red Oak, Latimer County, Indian Territory, United States
Occupation: U.S. Army First Choctaw and Chickasaw Mounted Rifles, 1861-1865
Married: Swega "Betsy" LeFlore. She was born in 1818, Choctaw nation East. Died in 1891, Choctaw nation West Indian Territory, United States. Interred: Red Oak Cemetery, Red Oak, Oklahoma
Additional Information: Swega's Choctaw name was "Le Wah Ha".

Children of WILLIAM MCCURTAIN and SWEGA LEFLORE:

i)   **Fannie McCurtain**, who married UNKNOWN Adams
ii)   **George McCurtain**,
iii)   **Jane McCurtain**, who married UNKNOWN Collins
iv)   **Mary Ann McCurtain**,
v)   **Melissa McCurtain**,
vi)   **Minnie McCurtain**,
vii)   **Sampson McCurtain**,
viii)   **Sillas McCurtain**,
ix)   **Joshua McCurtain**, born May 1863, Indian Territory, twin to Rebecca McCurtain. Died May 15, 1915 in McAlester, Oklahoma. He has one known son, Thomas McCurtain, born June 1886, and well as a daughter, who married Joe Dickerson. The son is noted the local papers as being "killed with a rock" by his brother-in-law while he was drunk one night in September of 1913. Thomas married Lilly Going Bohanan, by whom the line continues through their son Silas G. McCurtain "Bug", who died in 1955 and had several children.

x)   **<u>Rebecca McCurtain</u>**, born Jan. 24, 1863, in the Indian
Territory. She died May 26, 1920, in Nashoba, Oklahoma,
United States of America. Rebecca is the twin of her brother
Joshua. She granted the land which Nolia Cemetery stands
on, and where she is laid to rest. Rebecca Married twice to
James Frank Darden in 1885, and then after his death in
1895 to Francis Marion Witt. She had eight children through
both men: Joseph (1890), William (1891), Minnie (1893),
Charley (1895), Mary Ann (1897), John (1929), Frances
(1928), and Jessie (1928).

Article IV:

The Cadet Line of Curtins in Ireland
1685-1830

It is difficult to discern the identity of some personages in the era prior to 1900, which makes the Curtin ancestry difficult to discern. Catholic Church records are nil, and the "Church of Ireland" records appear uninterested in the ongoings of the local peoples. The earliest legal record of the region is the 1766 British religious census, which was designated to measure the strength of Irish "Papists" by region. The Diocese of Cloyne was among those regions covered by the census. Problematically, the parishes' shape and names have been altered over the last three centuries, making a concise reading of the census difficult. Among those listed are several men with the given name "John Curtin", any of whom might be the oldest historical member of this line of the Clan Curtin. However, this first John Curtin, whoever he was, is as of yet, impossible to identify. There are multiple potential claimants, but none of them reside near the parish of Rathcoggan (also known as 'Charleville') nor in neighboring Newmarket, Shandrum or Churchtown. This is largely due to the state of Catholicism in Ireland, which remained illegal in practice for several decades following the census. The "old church" in Charleville, now an abandoned chapel in the church cemetery, was also empty at the time of the 1766 census. The nearest functioning church would be in Bruree. It is possible that John resided in another nearby parish, such as: Kilquane, Cooliney, Anglishdrinagh, Ardpatrick, Kilmalock, Doneraile, or Effin. However, these records remain confined to print copies in the national archives and are not accessible abroad.

Where the Curtins were before this period is a point of speculation. It is clear they did not reside in Charleville a century prior, as it was deemed a stronghold for the English political presence in the region. Indeed, the settlement was founded by the barbarous Lord Broghill, who was reputed to have a deep loathing for the local Irish population. The local Irish would later express their disapproval for his policies by burning down his mansion in the years after his death. It is likely that the Curtins resided in either: Newmarket, Kilmallock, Shandrum or Doneraile prior to their arrival in Charleville in the 1770's. These three towns appear to have large concentrations of the surname, which might be the primary stalk of this Curtin branch. However, since records of that period are slim to nil, it is unlikely that there will be much more information gathered from the 18th century. Of these, Newmarket in Co. Cork appears to be the frontrunner, as a separate branch of the Curtins who remained in Ireland claim to have ancient ties to the city.

What does survive, and is put into this record, is a mix ecclesiastical record, tax documents, random civic license, census documents, emigration/deportation notices, family traditions, and probably a fair share of hearsay. That is to say, there are vast stretches of family history that are supposed from the limited of information available. Obviously, there is no attempt at chicancery, as many of the individuals noted in this record are humble Irish peasants. By merit of their ancestry they might claim descent through Cormac Cas in legend, but the practical affairs of their lives were often politically and economically bleak. The limited accounts of their agrarian existence should be 'ipse dixit'.

The oldest known Curtin progenitor's Christian name is certain to be John. His best attested son is given a dual or middle name, unusual for the period. When it was employed by Irish families it was done so to differentiate with a living family member. Since no "Michael Curtin" appears in the 1766 census for Cork, it can be safely assumed that John must be the accurate praenomen. However, much beyond this inference, nothing else can be gathered about his life. Neither he, nor his son have ever been found in the local civic records, but only through the private records of the Curtins who still reside in Charleville.

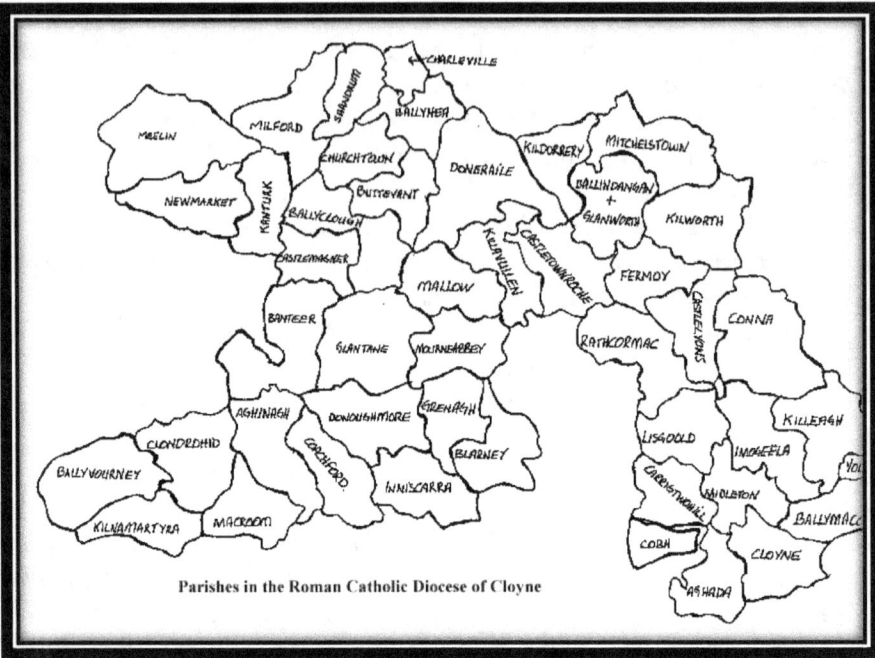

Parishes in the Roman Catholic Diocese of Cloyne

To confuse matters further, there does appear to be a number of Curtins who come into the region of Charleville as early as 1777, when Daniel Curtin appeared at the Old Church of the Holy Cross. His relationship to the rest of the genealogy appears vague. given the scarcity of the surname in Charleville at the time, he may be John Curtin's brother or less likely his son. There are also a number of women listed in the record as being married in town. Much like the origin of John Curtin, where they came from originally is unclear. Ecclesiastical records of this early period offer no name for the father of the bride. We can assume their relationships in this period solely because of the unlikely nature of distant travel and the relatively few Curtin families in and around Charleville.

Historical records for this early period are rare and, at times, unreliable. Most of church registries are limited to brief periods, some of which have been destroyed or are illegible from decay. To make matters worse, civil registration was not a requirement in Ireland until 1864, and many families simply did not bother to register the birth of a child with either church or state. The British government, for their part, maintained excellent records which they continue to hold for the purposes of bookkeeping. However, a careful review of these documents shows that no Curtin of this line was ever in the employ of the British civil service, army, or had anything to do with the alleged "Church of Ireland". This is perhaps heartening on a nationalistic level, but deeply frustrating as a matter of genealogical research.

To date, the oldest document regarding the early generation of Curtins in a headstone to the west of Charleville in the Ballinakill Cemetery. It makes note of the death of three Curtins, all of whom die within five years of one another. This has proven a miraculous starting point for the Curtins in the region, all the more so because the headstone is one of the few that is still legible after two centuries. What is not understood is why the headstone exists at all. From our terse understanding of the period, the Curtin family owned no land and possessed no trade. It seems likely that something significant must have happened to one or more of these individuals to elicit such a pricey response. If the matching of records is correct, it appears two-fold, the premature death of Daniel, and the deportation of John to Australia during the death of three of his relatives. What makes this headstone all the more perplexing is that it makes no references to "Michael J. Curtin". It might be presumed that he died much earlier, or after the erection of the monument.

an 18th century Irish homestead near Cork City

32b)   Bartholomew Curt(a)in,

son of Cornelius son of Phelim son of GiollaPadraig son of Eogan son of Eachmilidh son of Phelim son of Turlogh son of Aedh son of Eachmilidh son of Giolla Colm son of Giolla Droigin son of Giolla Domnall son of Giolla Padraig son of Searran son of Tomas Oge son of Tomas Mor son of Sean son of Donnchad of son of Giolla Colm son of Cinnait son of Eochaid son of Domnall son of Giolla Colm son of Ciannait son of Raghnall son of Searran son of Eochaidh son of Concruach MacArtán, son of Crum na-Cruach MacArtán, son of Cuonincon MacArtán, son of Artán

The lack of information that exists regarding the life of Bartholomew Curtain is perhaps symptomatic of the state of Irish Catholic in this epoch. Catholic Churches are demolished or repossessed by the state, marriage and baptismal records do not exist. There is little evidence to suggest that those who survived the Williamite War could make much of subsistence for themselves. Bartholomew stands out, as his name is unusual among the locals of the region. It is likely that his name is a function of his parentage, as we know his father Captain Cornelius Curtain took a second wife while serving in France. This would then render the date of his birth sometime after 1697 when this service to King James II was terminated. The name might be an intentional homage to St. Bartholomew's day, wherein French Catholics struck down the Protestant Huguenots. Beyond this reference among the Captain's children, he is again cited by the 1766 census of the Diocese of Cloyne. At this point in his life he is elderly, and these years between these two episodes are a mystery. However, his presence in this census does grant us the insight that he was head of household, and that he was not impoverished to the point of being ignored by the census board, as many tenant farmer families were. The scarcity of his name makes identification easy. Yet, it is unclear if he is the same Bartholomew Curtin who is residing in Boston and takes Katherine Guard for wife sometime in December of 1748.

> **Born:** later 17th century, early 18th century, in Northern Co. Cork, perhaps on August 23
> **Died:** after 1766, Northern Co. Cork, Ireland
> **Occupation:** Tenant Famer, (?) Innkeeper
> **Married:** Mary O'Sullivan, likely somewhere in Northern Cork.

Children of BARTHOLOMEW CURTAIN and MARY O'SULLIVAN:

i.   **Cornelius Curtain**, born about 1725. (*See Generation 33c*)
ii.   **William Curtain**, born about 1725. He might be the 'William Curtane' who was deported to America in 1742. The Curtins residing around the city of Washington DC in the 19th century were among his descendants. Allegedly they were involved in the construction of the White House. However, this identification is uncertain as penal records do not specify points of origin, only indicating that this William was arrested somewhere in county Limerick.
iii.   **John Curtain**, born about 1730 (*See Generation 33e below*)
iv.   **Mary Curtain,** beyond her name nothing else is noted regarding her life.
v.   **Bartholomew Curtain,** it is unclear whether it is this Bartholomew or his father that resided in Boston Massachusetts in the 1740's. Of the two Bartholomew's, father and son, he is more likely to have emigrated to Boston. Another marriage is recorded by the city of Boston between Bartholomew Curtain and Elenor Magee on Dec. 19, 1763. Given the proximity of the two marriages, they are likely to belong to the same man. He is likely the father or ancestor of Cornelius Curtin (1784-1859), Sally/Sarah Curtain, and Susan Curtin (1783-?).

Ursula Feore recalls a story told by her grandfather, Thomas Feore, wife of Mary Ann Curtin. He indicated that Curtins were sent to America to work on the White House under the Irish Catholic architect, James Hoban. However, she cannot recall any further detail. This story is intriguing, as the US Census of 1790 and 1800 indicate two construction workers Dennis and Edward Curtain residing in Prince George's County in Maryland, just outside of the city limits of Washington DC. They are the children of a certain "William Curtane", a native of Ireland, who was sent to the American colonies in 1742 for "vagabondry and sedition" having been captured while in Co Limerick. No other information is currently available. It appears likely that William is related to John (Generation IIIb), but further research is needed to clarify the nature of their relationship.

Irish Coin from the reign of King George III

33e)   John Curt(a)in,

son of Bartholomew son of Cornelius son of Phelim son of GiollaPadraig son of Eogan son of Eachmilidh son of Phelim son of Turlogh son of Aedh son of Eachmilidh son of Giolla Colm son of Giolla Droigin son of Giolla Domnall son of Giolla Padraig son of Searran son of Tomas Oge son of Tomas Mor son of Sean son of Donnchad of son of Giolla Colm son of Cinnait son of Eochaid son of Domnall son of Giolla Colm son of Ciannait son of Raghnall son of Searran son of Eochaidh son of Concruach MacArtán, son of Crum na-Cruach MacArtán, son of Cuonincon MacArtán, son of Artán

It is likely that he appears in the 1766 census for the Diocese of Cloyne. However, because of changes to the boundaries of parishes, it is impossible to determine which John Curtin he is. He does not appear as a resident of Charleville proper, nor does any Curtin, as the townland had been mostly repossessed two generations prior and redistributed to Protestant families. It appears that these earlier Curtins must have resided close enough to town to be part of the parish, but not the civil district of Charleville proper.

> **Born**: around 1730 or so, near Rathcoggan (but not in it), possibly Newmarket, Co. Cork, Ireland
> **Died**: Unknown, probably Newmarket, Co. Cork, Ireland
> **Occupation**: Unknown, likely tenant farmer

Children of JOHN CURTIN and UNKNOWN
i.   **Daniel Curtin**, birth: around 1755, Newmarket, Co. Cork, Kingdom of Ireland
        (*Section IXb below*)

ii. **Michael J. Curtin**, birth: around 1760, Newmarket, Co. Cork, Kingdom of Ireland
(Section IXc below)

iii. **Mary Curtin**, birth after 1770, Newmarket, Co. Cork, Kingdom of Ireland
Died: (Unknown)
Married: Nov. 22, 1802 at (Old) Church of the Holy Cross, Charleville, Co. Cork, Ireland
Husband: James McAuliffe; it is unknown   whether she had children or not as the ecclesiastical records are missing for three decades in the parish of Charleville.

33c) Cornelius Curt(a)in,

son of Bartholomew son of Cornelius son of Phelim son of GiollaPadraig son of Eogan son of Eachmilidh son of Phelim son of Turlogh son of Aedh son of Eachmilidh son of Giolla Colm son of Giolla Droigin son of Giolla Domnall son of Giolla Padraig son of Searran son of Tomas Oge son of Tomas Mor son of Sean son of Donnchad of son of Giolla Colm son of Cinnait son of Eochaid son of Domnall son of Giolla Colm son of Ciannait son of Raghnall son of Searran son of Eochaidh son of Concruach MacArtán, son of Crum na-Cruach MacArtán, son of Cuonincon MacArtán, son of Artán

Little is known regarding the life of this Cornelius, as records from the 18th century are few and far between. He does appear in the religious census of 1766 and is said to have resided near the Kilcascan District. He descendants appear in and around the townland of Mallow. Given that his ancestors resided likewise, it might be presumed that he remained near Mallow during his lifetime.

Born: around 1725
Died: after 1766
Occupation: Farmer, possibly landowner(?)
Married: Mary Donnelly

Children of CORNELIUS CURTIN and MARY DONNELLY:

i   **Bartholomew Curtin**, died young.
ii.   **Mary Curtin**, fate unknown.
iii.   **Thomas Curtin**, perhaps mentioned as residing nearby in the parish of Kilsahnnig in the 1766 census.
iv.   **John Curtin**, (*See Generation 34d below*)

34d)   John Curtin,

son of Cornelius son of Bartholomew son of Cornelius son of Phelim son of GiollaPadraig son of Eogan son of Eachmilidh son of Phelim son of Turlogh son of Aedh son of Eachmilidh son of Giolla Colm son of Giolla Droigin son of Giolla Domnall son of Giolla Padraig son of Searran son of Tomas Oge son of Tomas Mor son of Sean son of Donnchad of son of Giolla Colm son of Cinnait son of Eochaid son of Domnall son of Giolla Colm son of Ciannait son of Raghnall son of Searran son of Eochaidh son of Concruach MacArtán, son of Crum na-Cruach MacArtán, son of Cuonincon MacArtán, son of Artán

Like his father, John lived through a dark period in Irish records and little has survived regarding his lifetime. Two sons are known, no daughters and no wife appear in family records. No state or church records survive.

> **Born:** around 1750, likely near Mallow, Co. Cork, Kingdom of Ireland
> **Died:** unknown
> **Occupation:** Farmer, possibly landowner(?)
> **Married:** Unknown

Children of JOHN CURTIN and UNKNOWN
i.   **Cornelius Curtin**, (*See Generation 35d below in Article V*)
ii.   **Dennis Curtin**, born about 1780. Killed in the Pikemens' rebellion in 1798 in hope of a French invasion of Ireland. In a rare state record, he is recorded as being a farmer from Gurtmore, who made a Catholic Oath of Allegiance at Mallow, Cork on April 14, 1796.

The Rockite Rebellion tore through Northern County Cork in this generation. We know from the records of the Royal Irish Constabulary (RIC) that the Curtin family was involved, but this involvement seems befuddled by the limited number of records available. At least two members of the family appear to have been formally charged with treason in association with Captain Rock. Their involvement seems intimately tied to the leadership of the rebellion, which may have been strengthened through familial ties. Perhaps what is most curious is the existence of a Cornelius Curtin of Gortnaskehy, who testifies again Thomas Hoskins, claiming that he is the true identity of the anonymous 'Captain Rock'. The Cork papers report that his fields were burnt at night in retaliation by United Irishmen in November of 1823. It might be questioned how Cornelius had this information. However, time and domestic policies of the British Empire have eradicated the few recorded memories of this event.

The Rockite Rebellion swept through rural Ireland from 1822 to 1824, enlisting families such as: the Feores, the Hickeys, and the Curtins.

34e)   Daniel Curt(a)in,

son of John son of Bartholomew son of Cornelius son of Phelim son of GiollaPadraig son of Eogan son of Eachmilidh son of Phelim son of Turlogh son of Aedh son of Eachmilidh son of Giolla Colm son of Giolla Droigin son of Giolla Domnall son of Giolla Padraig son of Searran son of Tomas Oge son of Tomas Mor son of Sean son of Donnchad of son of Giolla Colm son of Cinnait son of Eochaid son of Domnall son of Giolla Colm son of Ciannait son of Raghnall son of Searran son of Eochaidh son of Concruach MacArtán, son of Crum na-Cruach MacArtán, son of Cuonincon MacArtán, son of Artán

Daniel appears in a brief moment of transition, as the Curtins appear to be slowly being pulled to Charleville as a local cultural hub. This is also reflected in Charleville's shifting demographics, moving from an English Protestant township to an Irish Catholic one. Of Daniel's life, very little can be said that is not outlined below.

> **Born:** around 1755, Newmarket, Co. Cork, Kingdom of Ireland
> **Died:** (Unknown)
> **Occupation:** (Unknown)
> **Married:** ANASTASIA HICKEY, (Old) Church of the Holy Cross, Charleville, Co. Cork, Ireland on July 22, 1777. She is noted in the registry as not being of the parish. Most likely she is a resident of Doneraile.

Children of DANIEL CURTIN and ANASTASIA HICKEY:

i.   **John Curtin**, born: 1788/1792/1793/1794, Charleville, Co. Cork, Kingdom of Ireland
Australian Deportation: arrived August 12, 1823, on board the "Isabella", 7-year term. Given bill of leave on August 18, 1828. Never issued bill of freedom.
Occupation: "Reaper"/"Labourer"
Australia Census 1828: 35 years old, Catholic, residing in Bathurst
Died: 1829, Abercrombie District, Bathurst, Australia
Additional Notes: He appears to have been involved in the "Rockite insurrection" in 1823, a sub-branch of the Whiteboy rebels, with accomplices: Timothy Buckley, John Crowe, Edmond Madigan, and John Sheedy. They broke into the Charleville prison and released those captives there. He was 5'4 according to the record and must have had a heavy accent as his home town is noted as "Charleywell". The name of his mother is curious as well. "Captain Rock", the supposed leader of the rebellion was believed to be a man named John Hickey, who was a native of the neighboring town of Doneraile. While no genealogical of Captain Rock survives, it seems likely that this John was a close familial relation to him given the scarcity of the surname.

ii.   **Daniel Curtin**, only referenced in the marriage record of his cousin of the same name in 1830. Nothing else is known about his life or later whereabouts.

34e)   'Michael' Joseph Curt(a)in,

*son of John son of Bartholomew son of Cornelius son of Phelim son of
GiollaPadraig son of Eogan son of Eachmilidh son of Phelim son of Turlogh son of
Aedh son of Eachmilidh son of Giolla Colm son of Giolla Droigin son of Giolla
Domnall son of Giolla Padraig son of Searran son of Tomas Oge son of Tomas Mor
son of Sean son of Donnchad of son of Giolla Colm son of Cinnait son of Eochaid
son of Domnall son of Giolla Colm son of Ciannait son of Raghnall son of Searran
son of Eochaidh son of Concruach MacArtán, son of Crum na-Cruach MacArtán,
son of Cuonincon MacArtán, son of Artán*

His middle name is a point of contention. He likely is synonymous with the
"Michael Joseph Curtin" who was also heavily involved in the Rockite
rebellion. The latter holds weight, as it would explain his absence from his
family's burial plot in Ballinakill. If this is true, he would have been 63 years
old at the time of his death. Moreover, if his brother is correctly identified,
then this appears to be a common political thread throughout the Curtin family
of the 18th and 19th centuries. During his early life he appears to be a literate
servant working for the Power Family in Charleville. This was an Anglo-Irish
family which has ties to the Church of Ireland and to the Irish Peerage.
Michael's wife, Ellen, is likely a member of this house. However, her marriage
to a native Irish Catholic would make her estranged from her relatives.
However, this may be providentially why she, and not Michael, was given a
headstone in Ballinakill Cemetery. His dual name is not explained and there
are no church records to secure what he was baptized. The oral tradition

surrounding him claims that he was born a "Joseph". He had been conscripted into the American War for Independence, wherein he abandoned the army and attempted to escape into Upper Canada where he was apprehended by local British authorities. While he was incarcerated, he had a vision of the Archangel Michael, who helped him escape. Thereafter, he re-christened himself Michael-Joseph following his escape. This episode does seem to mimic the events of Acts 16:16-40, wherein St. Paul is freed from jail by an angelic being, this seems to make this folktale appear somewhat dubious.

Born: 1758/1759, Newmarket (?), Co. Cork, Kingdom of Ireland
Died: 1823 or thereabouts, perhaps during the Rockite rebellion itself
Occupation: Some minor estate secretary (?), tenant farmer
Married: ELLEN POWER, possibly July 1, 1788(?), (Old) Church of the Holy Cross, Charleville, Co. Cork, Ireland
1st Wife: ELLEN POWER, born 1762, died: January 16, 1825, Charleville, Co. Cork, Ireland. interred: Ballinakill Cemetery, Charleville, Co. Cork. Daughter of WILLIAM POWER and UNKNOWN.

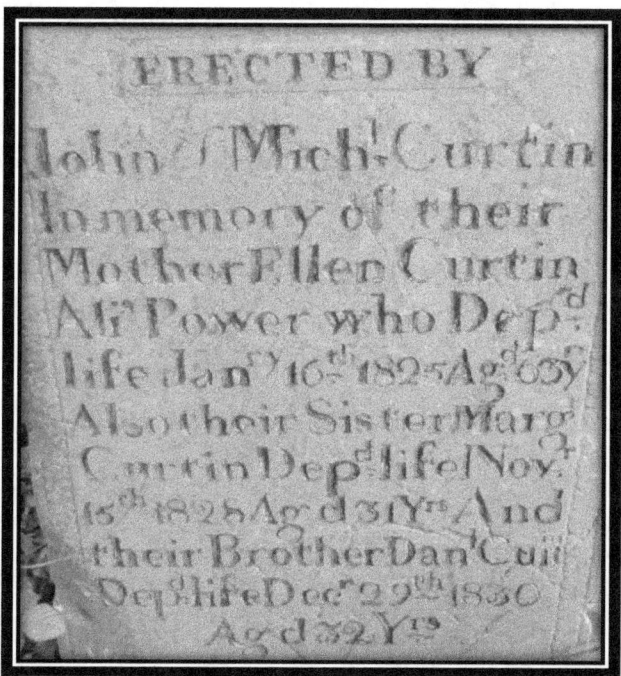

The headstone of Margaret, Daniel and Ellen Curtin. This is the only known moment of a Curtin in Ireland that survives to the present day.

Children of MICHAEL J. CURTIN and ELLEN POWER

i.   **John Curtin**, born: 1790's, Newmarket, Co. Cork, Kingdom of Ireland. John has various descendants who initially resided around the Newmarket area, with immigration to both Canada and the United States in later generations.

ii.   **Daniel Curtin**, born 1798, Newmarket, Co. Cork, Kingdom of Ireland. His patrilineal descendants continue only in America through the immigration of his grandson Michael Francis Curtin (born 1875). These Curtins remain around the Philadelphia area to this day.

iii. **Margaret Curtin**, born 1799, Newmarket, Co. Cork, Kingdom of Ireland
      Died: November 15, 1828, Charleville, Co. Cork, Ireland; interred: Ballinakill Cemetery, Charleville, Co. Cork, Ireland
      Additional Notes: She appears to be a spinster at the time of her death at the age of twenty-nine.

iv.   **Michael Curtin**, born 1800(?), Newmarket, Co. Cork, Kingdom of Ireland. These Curtins remain in the Kanturk/Charleville area and continue to employ the name Michael, every subsequent generation to the present day.

v.   **Timothy Curtin**, nothing else is noted of his existence beyond his name as it appears in a Curtin genealogy presented by Tim Curtin.

vi.   **William Curtin (?)**, this individual is entirely hypothetical as no records of him exist. However, it seems likely that a boy named William must have been alive at some point, as the second male son is frequently named for his maternal grandfather. If this is true, he would have been dead before 1830.

Article V:
"Advance Australia Fair!"
Later Curtins of Australia
1823-1945

35d) Cornelius Curtin,

son of John son of Cornelius son of Bartholomew son of Cornelius son of Phelim son of GiollaPadraig son of Eogan son of Eachmilidh son of Phelim son of Turlogh son of Aedh son of Eachmilidh son of Giolla Colm son of Giolla Droigin son of Giolla Domnall son of Giolla Padraig son of Searran son of Tomas Oge son of Tomas Mor son of Sean son of Donnchad of son of Giolla Colm son of Cinnait son of Eochaid son of Domnall son of Giolla Colm son of Ciannait son of Raghnall son of Searran son of Eochaidh son of Concruach MacArtán, son of Crum na-Cruach MacArtán, son of Cuonincon MacArtán, son of Artán

There a several traces in land tithing books regarding Cornelius' life, which stands in contrast to all of his ancestors in the 18th century. In the tithe books he is said to possess 12 acres in Upper Kilpadder, near Mallow and Kanturk. He may have experiencing conscription during the Napoleonic wars into the British military.

> **Born:** 1780, likely near Mallow, Co. Cork, Kingdom of Ireland
> **Died:** 1864, Kanturk, Co. Cork, Ireland, United Kingdom
> **Occupation:** Farmer, landowner
> **Married:** Mary McKerig, likely around 1800. Her headstone survives in the Newberry cemetery, near the township of Mallow. She is said to have died age 40, on June 24, 1817. She might be the daughter of Cornelius McKearin of Banteer.

> Children of JOHN CURTIN and MARY MCKERIG
> i.   **John Cornelius Curtin**, *(See Generation 36a below)* born around 1800, the only child of both parents.

36a)   John Cornelius Curtin,

*son of Cornelius son of John son of Cornelius son of Bartholomew son of Cornelius
son of Phelim son of GiollaPadraig son of Eogan son of Eachmilidh son of Phelim
son of Turlogh son of Aedh son of Eachmilidh son of Giolla Colm son of Giolla
Droigin son of Giolla Domnall son of Giolla Padraig son of Searran son of Tomas
Oge son of Tomas Mor son of Sean son of Donnchad of son of Giolla Colm son of
Cinnait son of Eochaid son of Domnall son of Giolla Colm son of Ciannait son of
Raghnall son of Searran son of Eochaidh son of Concruach MacArtán, son of
Crum na-Cruach MacArtán, son of Cuonincon MacArtán, son of Artán*

John appears to have held stronger financial dealings than all previous
generations going back two centuries. According through Griffith's Land
Evaluation in 1853, he held 46 acres in Kilpadder (which remains with the
Curtin family today). He appears to have been active in his Catholic parish in
Kilshanig during his lifetime.

> **Born:** about 1800, Kanturk, Co. Cork, Kingdom of Ireland
> **Died:** 1873, Kanturk, Co. Cork, United Kingdom
> **Occupation:** Farmer, landowner
> **Married:** Mary Hanlon, married February 2, 1837, Donaghmore, Co.
> Cork, Ireland, United Kingdom. She was a native to Donaghmore, the
> daughter of Denis Hanlon and Joan Connors. She died in 1876 at age
> 60 and is believed to have been buried in the Roman catholic
> cemetery in Kanturk. If she had a headstone erected it no longer
> stands.

> Children of JOHN CORENLIUS CURTIN and MARY HANLON:
> i.   **Mary Ann Curtin**, born December 21, 1837, died 1921.
> ii.   **Cornelius Curtin**, born July 2, 1840, Gloutane, Co. Cork,
>   died 1931. The eldest son who appears to have inherited the
>   farm from his father upon his death. He had nine children,
>   and it is among his descendants that run and maintain the
>   large farm in Kilpadder to this day.
> iii.   **Dennis Curtin**, born May 18, 1843, Gloutane, Co. Cork.
>   Died 1917. Dennis married Bridget Conway in Adelaide,
>   South Australia in 1876. Thereafter, they moved to
>   Melbourne in Victoria. They had one son, John Michael
>   Curtin, who was born in 1879. Bridget died in 1882 and
>   Dennis and his son returned to Ireland. Dennis is buried in
>   Kanturk at the Newberry Cemetery. His son John is buried
>   in Drishane Cemetery.
> iv.   **Johannah Curtin**, April 19, 1846, Mallow, Co. Cork. Died
>   1939.

v.   **Michael John Curtin,** November 27, 1850, Mallow, Co. Cork. Died June 1921. He emigrated to Australia, where he married Margaret Kain in 1882, and had many children, of whom his descendants survive to this day.

vi.   **John Curtin,** born January 29, 1853, Kilpadder, Co. Cork

vi.   **Bridget Curtin,** born May 17, 1855, Gloutane. Co. Cork, died in 1946.

36a)   John Cornelius Curtin,

son of Cornelius son of John son of Cornelius son of Bartholomew son of Cornelius son of Phelim son of GiollaPadraig son of Eogan son of Eachmilidh son of Phelim son of Turlogh son of Aedh son of Eachmilidh son of Giolla Colm son of Giolla Droigin son of Giolla Domnall son of Giolla Padraig son of Searran son of Tomas Oge son of Tomas Mor son of Sean son of Donnchad of son of Giolla Colm son of Cinnait son of Eochaid son of Domnall son of Giolla Colm son of Ciannait son of Raghnall son of Searran son of Eochaidh son of Concruach MacArtán, son of Crum na-Cruach MacArtán, son of Cuonincon MacArtán, son of Artán

John owned 46 acres in Kilpadder according the Griffith Evaluation of 1853.This places him in a rare position for Irish Catholic farmers, as the vast majority were blocked from owning their farmland. It is possible that this farmland is a fragment of the estate of Capt. Cornelius Curtain from the late 17th century. Regardless, he would have been among the higher socio-economic echelon of 19th century Ireland.

Born: abt. 1800, likely Kanturk, Co. Cork, Kingdom of Ireland
Died: 1873, Kanturk, Co. Cork, Ireland,
Occupation: non-tenant farmer
Married: MARY HANLON, February 2, 1837, Donaghmore, Co. Cork, Ireland

Children of JOHN CORNELIUS CURTIN and MARY HANLON are:

i.   **Mary Ann Curtin**, born December 21, 1837, Gloutane, Cork, died 1921

ii.   **Cornelius Curtin**, born July 2, 1840, Gloutane, Co. Cork, died 1931. He had nine children of his own, of whom his great-grandson Denis Curtin still owns and operates the family farm.

iii.   **Dennis Curtin**, born May 18, 1843, Gloutane, Co. Cork, died 1917

iv.   **Johannah Curtin**, born April 19, 1846, Gloutane, Co. Cork, died 1939

v.   **Michael John Curtin**, born November 27, 1850, Gloutane, Co. Cork, died June 1921, Southern Australia

vi.   **John Curtin**, born January 1, 1853, Kilpadder-Gloutane, Co. Cork, died 1919 (*See Generation 37a below*)

vii.   **Bridget Curtin**, born May 5, 1855, Gloutane, Co. Cork, died 1946

37a) John Curtin (Jr.),

Son of John son of Cornelius son of John son of Cornelius son of Bartholomew son of Cornelius son of Phelim son of GiollaPadraig son of Eogan son of Eachmilidh son of Phelim son of Turlogh son of Aedh son of Eachmilidh son of Giolla Colm son of Giolla Droigin son of Giolla Domnall son of Giolla Padraig son of Searran son of Tomas Oge son of Tomas Mor son of Sean son of Donnchad of son of Giolla Colm son of Cinnait son of Eochaid son of Domnall son of Giolla Colm son of Ciannait son of Raghnall son of Searran son of Eochaidh son of Concruach MacArtán, son of Crum na-Cruach MacArtán, son of Cuonincon MacArtán, son of Artán

He joined the British Army around 1870, where he gave service to the British Army in India. Thereafter, he followed his brother to Australia in 1880 after securing employment with the Victorian Police service. He was stationed at Creswick from 1881 to 1890. Following the deterioration of his physical health, he left the service, entering into the hospitality industry and managing hotels in the region. Because of the limitation of his working schedule the family delved into poverty, and was eventually forced to settle in Brunswick, Australia. John suffered from chronic rheumatoid arthritis, and late in life ran a pub in Brunswick on Little Lonsdale Street.

Born: January 27, 1853, Kilshanning, Co. Cork, Ireland
Died: March 25, 1919, Melbourne, Dominion of Australia
Married: KATHERINE AGNES BOURKE, June 6, 1883, St. Patrick's Cathedral, Melbourne, Colony of Australia

Children of JOHN CURTIN and KATHERINE BOURKE are:

i.   **John Joseph Ambrose Curtin**, born January 8, 1885 in Creswick, died in 1945.

ii.   **George William Curtin**, born March 15, 1887 in Creswick, died in 1959. He married Elsie Emma Dyson.

iii.   **Mary Ellen Curtin**, born in 1889 in Creswick, Colony of Australia, died in 1971 in St. Kilda, Victoria, Dominion of Australia. She married a gentleman with the surname 'White'.

iv.   **Hannah Francis Curtin**, born 1892 in Dandringham, died in April 23, 1946. She married Peter J. Curtin, who despite the surname, was not a relative.

38a)   John Joseph Ambrose Curtin,

Son of John son of John son of Cornelius son of John son of Cornelius son of Bartholomew son of Cornelius son of Phelim son of GiollaPadraig son of Eogan son of Eachmilidh son of Phelim son of Turlogh son of Aedh son of Eachmilidh son of Giolla Colm son of Giolla Droigin son of Giolla Domnall son of Giolla Padraig son of Searran son of Tomas Oge son of Tomas Mor son of Sean son of Donnchad of son of Giolla Colm son of Cinnait son of Eochaid son of Domnall son of Giolla Colm son of Ciannait son of Raghnall son of Searran son of Eochaidh son of Concruach MacArtán, son of Crum na-Cruach MacArtán, son of Cuonincon MacArtán, son of Artán

**14th Prime Minister of Australia:
October 7, 1941- July 5, 1945
Australian Minister for Defense: October 7, 1941- July 5, 1945
MP for Fremantle: September 15, 1934- July 5, 1945**

John is, perhaps, the most of famous of all the Curtins on the world stage, and he is a fitting end point for this book of genealogy, as he achieves what would otherwise be impossible. He gives the greatest compliments to the English invaders of Ireland by rising through their colonial ranks to achieve the highest office in the land, albeit one on a foreign shore. Because of his fame, there I a tremendous amount written about this man of the people who has become integral to the history of Australia politics.

John was born in Creswick, Victoria. His family christened him "John Joseph Ambrose Curtin", although these later ecclesiastical names were never used later in life. He was commonly known as 'Jack' to his friends and family. He was born with a significant ocular disorder (congenital strabismus) in his left eye, which he had throughout his lifetime. John became increasingly involved in Australia's Labor Party starting in during the First World War and being strongly encouraged by his wife, Elsie. John's political career was heavily tied to the rights and dignity of workers and in the protection of children. He would lead Australia through the military campaigns of the Second World War protecting the continent from Japanese expansionist aggression. He remains a pivotal figure in the history of Australia and has a variety of institutions named in his honor- including that of Curtin University. His statute stands outside of Freemantle townhall, and the 2007 film 'Curtin' regards his life and accomplishments.

Born: January 8, 1885, Creswick, Colony of Victoria
Died: July 5, 1945, Canberra, ACT, Dominion of Australia; interred: Karrakatta Cemetery, Perth, Dominion of Australia.
Education: St. Francis' Boys School, St. Bridget's School, Macedon Primary School ?-1894
Occupation: Office Boy- The Rambler Magazine 1899-1900, Copy Boy- The Age (Newspaper), Houseboy at a Gentlemen's Club. Clerk- Titan Manufacturing Company 1903-1911, State Secretary- Timberworkers' Union 1911-1915, President- Timberworkers' Union 1915-1917, Editor-Westralian Worker 1917-1935, Leader of the Labor Party 1935-1945, MP for Fremantle 1934-1945, Minister of Defense 1941-1945, 14th Prime Minister of Australia 1941-1945

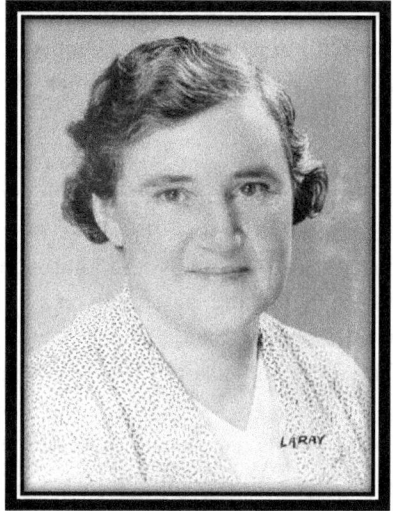

Married: ELSIE NEEDHAM, daughter of ABRHAM NEEDHAM and ANNIE HOSKING, born October 4, 1890, Ballarat, Colony of Victoria, died June 24, 1975, Perth, Western Australia, Dominion of Australia. Married April 21, 1917 in Perth, Dominion of Australia. Elsie grew up in Cape Town, South African Republic until 1910. She moved to Hobart in Tasmania where she met John Curtin. Late in life she was named a Commander of the British Empire.

Children of JOHN J. CURTIN and ELSIE NEEDHAM are:

   i)   **John Francis Curtin,** born January 31, 1921, later became a Sergeant in the Royal Australian Air Force (RAAF). John married Catherine Reid Neill at the Ross Memorial

Presbyterian Church in Perth on December 9, 1944 by Rev. J. Aitkin. John died June 20, 2007 and was buried at Karrakatta Cemetery with his parents. He was the father of two children, John and Barbara.

ii)   **Elsie Milda Curtin**, born December 30, 1917, Perth, Western Australia. She married Stan MacLeod in 1948. She died in the city of her birth on May 5, 2009 and was interred at Karrakatta Cemetery with her family.

www.ingramcontent.com/pod-product-compliance
Lightning Source LLC
Chambersburg PA
CBHW071102120626
46546CB00003B/1246